Hallelujah Holiday Recipes

From God's Garden

HALLELUJAH ACRES

Brings you back to the Garden

Hallelujah Holiday Recipes…from God's Garden

The nutritional and health information in this book is based on the teachings of God's Holy Word, the Bible, as well as research and personal experiences by the author and many others. The purpose of this book is to provide information and education about health. The author and publisher do not offer medical advice or prescribe the use of diet as a form or treatment for sickness without the approval of a health professional.

Because there is always some risk involved when changing diet and lifestyles, the author and publisher are not responsible for any adverse effects or consequences that might result. Please do not apply the techniques of this book if you are not willing to assume the risk.

If you do use the information contained in this book without the approval of a health professional, you are prescribing for yourself, which is your constitutional right, but the author and publisher assume no responsibility.

© Copyright 2005 by Rhonda J. Malkmus
All rights reserved
Library of Congress in Publication Data
Malkmus, Rhonda J.
Hallelujah Holiday Recipes … from God's Garden
1. Christian, 2. Recipes, 3. Health, 4. Raw Food
Library of Congress Catalog Card Number

Layout and Design by Shannon Brown (AdvanceGraphics.us)

ISBN 0-929619-22-6

First Printing 2005
Printed in the United States of America
All Bible quotations are taken from the authorized King James Version

Published and Distributed by
Hallelujah Acres Publishing
PO Box 2388
Shelby, NC 28151
704.481.1700

Visit our website at www.hacres.com.

Dedication

This book is dedicated to all the wonderful people who have made a difference in my life!

It is dedicated in memory of my precious earthly father, Ellsworth Eugene Brandow, who went home to be with the Lord on October 24, 2003, and my beloved mother, Eleanor Ruth Fraser Brandow. After 60+ years of marriage, their selfless dedication to their family is a great example to all who know them!

It is dedicated to my precious husband, George Malkmus, who is my mentor, my partner, and my hero! He is always by my side encouraging me to press toward the mark. I never cease to be amazed by his patience when I'm working on a book for you. There are times he may not see the whites of my eyes for endless hours and yet he never complains!

This book is also dedicated:

To the rest of my family, who live hundreds of miles away, but are always an encouragement to me. They inspire me with their never-ending love and understanding!

To my awesome friends, who motivate me with their support, their prayers, and their love.

To the staff at Hallelujah Acres® who tirelessly give of themselves to help others reach their goal of Ultimate Health on an ongoing basis.

To our wonderful Health Ministers℠ around the world who never tire of helping us reach the world with the message, "you don't have to be sick!"

To all who follow the Hallelujah Diet and Lifestyle℠ and are regaining their health, and to those who are saving their very lives by the choices they make.

Last, but certainly not least, to our Lord and Saviour, Jesus Christ, that He might be lifted up, and that you may know Him as your personal Saviour.

"Grace be unto you, and peace, from God our Father, and
from the Lord Jesus Christ. I thank my God
upon every remembrance of you,..."

—Philippians 1:2-3

Acknowledgements

I give thanks with a grateful heart:

To my Lord and Saviour, Jesus Christ, who through the power of the Holy Spirit, gave me the vision to create these Holiday Recipes and the strength and vision to complete this work.

To my beloved husband, George, who always encourages me to give my best for God's service! His patience and understanding are my strength! It is such a joy to share his vision that some day, in some way, the whole world might know *"You Don't Have to be Sick!"* ℠ Without George and The Hallelujah Diet®, I'd be in a sorry state of health today, maybe even in a wheelchair! Instead, George and I climb mountains together and will continue to do so for there is much to be done; the fields are "white unto harvest!"

To the staff of Hallelujah Acres® for their tireless efforts to help us reach the world with not only the health message but the gospel as well. They toil behind the scenes and make all that we do at Hallelujah Acres® seem effortless. Their efforts don't go unnoticed, for they are deeply appreciated!

To my friends, from around the world, who have encouraged me and submitted recipes to be used in this book; their contributions help to create the endless ideas and creativity found in this book.

To all of those who have done an excellent job of editing and proofreading these recipes and given of their valuable time and energies to make this dream become a reality. Without their efforts none of this would have been possible…to God be the Glory!

"I thank my God always on your behalf, for the grace of God which is given you by Jesus Christ; That in every thing ye are enriched by Him, in all utterance, and in all knowledge; Even as the testimony of Christ was confirmed in you:"

—1 Corinthians 1:4–6

Caution: The Choice Is Yours

As the reader will soon realize, several of the recipes that are contained in this book have been submitted by some of our *Back to the Garden Newsletter*℠ and *Hallelujah Health Tip*® readers.

Some recipes may contain some ingredients that are not ideal. Readers will need to judge for themselves whether the ingredients in each recipe are something they would like to use. Substitutions can be made, or ingredients can be omitted, reduced, or increased to suit the taste buds and preferences of each individual or family.

We use a "five-star" rating system to help you determine the recipes that are most appropriate for your dietary and lifestyle goals. While even our "five-star" recipes are all raw and properly combined, we would encourage anyone dealing with chronic degenerative conditions such as cancer and heart disease to carefully consider eliminating or minimizing the use of even raw nuts, seeds, and most unrefined oils with the exception of either flaxseed oil or Udo's oil (if dealing with prostate cancer, freshly ground flaxseed may be a better option than either of these oils).

We encourage the reader to experiment, make substitutions, and find out what is most pleasing to your palate. This is an adventure that can change your life forever—each new step you take can assist you in attaining and sustaining "Ultimate Health." May our Lord and Saviour, Jesus Christ, bless and guide you and those you love as you seek to change your diet and lifestyle so that each of you, too, can sustain or renew your strength and be able soar like the eagle!

"Thou shalt come to thy grave in a full age, like as a shock of corn cometh in in his season."

—Job 5:26

By The Grace Of God

In 1981 an event happened, in the twinkling of an eye, which changed my life forever! It changed how I think, what is important to me and who I am! On a rainy, foggy night, I was driving along a rural road in Iowa. As my car approached an unmarked railroad crossing, my passenger yelled, "Oh my God, there's a train!" I slammed on the brakes and my car screeched to a halt and stalled inches from the railroad crossing. Realizing we were too close to the track, I took my foot off the brake to try to restart the engine and when I did, the car inched ever closer to the path of the oncoming train. Frantically, I tried to restart my car but to no avail. There we were with no time to escape; I truly expected to meet the Lord that night.

After the initial impact, the car flew through the air. When the car landed and finally stopped rolling, the very first thought I had was, "In everything give thanks: for this is the will of God in Christ Jesus concerning you" (I Thessalonians 5:18). With fear and trembling, I thanked the Lord as my hand landed on the window crank. The train engineer had already run to my car, and I called to him to open the door, but he was in shock and thought we were dead so he simply stood there staring. Imagine his reaction when I rolled down the window and climbed out of the car and then opened the door and helped my passenger to safety. By the Grace of God, my friend and I walked away from a potentially deadly accident!

We were rushed to the hospital where we received many x-rays. The doctors were amazed that they could find no broken bones, only cracked ribs, a spine that was way out of alignment, one small laceration, and many bruises. However, in the days, weeks, and months that followed, I learned what an impact with a freight train can do to the human body. My fillings were shattered as well as the enamel on many of my teeth. As a result of the accident, I began to develop arthritis in every joint of my body.

Almost overnight, pain had become my constant companion. Often the pain was so intense that there were days I thought going to heaven would have been easier than living. If I sat in a chair, I could hardly get up; if I stood any length of time, I could hardly sit down. I had to run hot water on my hands each morning before doing anything else to get them to function. My right elbow, that had been dislocated, ached constantly as well as the contusion on my thigh caused by my knee going through the dash. There wasn't an area in my spine that wasn't affected. Due to the pain often being almost unbearable, I was relatively inactive and this brought many unwanted pounds. In my heart, I knew God allowed this accident to happen for a reason, I just didn't know "the rest of the story."

By the fall of 1990, the arthritis was so severe that my doctor advised that I move to milder climate. After having had my home on the market for four years, it finally sold. An answer to prayer as the offer I received was to the penny I had been praying for. When I arrived in Tennessee, the first person I met was George Malkmus! Meeting George was the second collision in my life! But this one would bring joy and the unveiling of God's purpose for my pain. George began to share with me that a changed diet and lifestyle would no doubt improve my life and health. With nothing to loose and everything to gain, I began to change my diet to The Hallelujah Diet® and over a period of time it truly did change my life. Today my health has been completely restored and I can now do things I could only dream about before. I am free of pain, walk two to eight miles daily on hilly terrain, and have lost over 80 pounds.

After experiencing the health a simple diet change can bring, HALLELUJAH is a most appropriate word. Over the past several years, over two million others have changed their diet and lifestyle to The Hallelujah Diet®, with many experiencing wonderful results. Our mission is to teach the world God's plan for our diet and health, and to share with others "*You Don't Have to be Sick!*"ᔆᴹ

(For more information on The Hallelujah Diet®, see our website and address on the back page.)

"The thief cometh not, but for to steal, and to kill, and to destroy: I am come that they might have life, and that they might have it more abundantly."

—*John 10:10*

Hallelujah Holiday Recipes

by Rhonda Malkmus and friends

"I beseech you therefore, brethren, by the mercies of God, that ye present your bodies a living sacrifice, holy, acceptable unto God, which is your reasonable service. And be not conformed to this world: but be ye transformed by the renewing of your mind, that ye may prove what is that good, and acceptable, and perfect, will of God."

—Romans 12:1–2

Over the years, many have asked, "What should we do for the holidays?" I've spent a lot of time in prayer asking the Lord to help me answer that question. This book is a result of many hours of prayer, and of course, your contributions. May it bring you and your family many wonderful memories to cherish!

Each year as family and friends gather for Thanksgiving, Christmas, and other holidays, the sounds of laughter and happy conversation fill the air. It is a time when hearts and homes are opened to share with one another. We relive memories of bygone days and anticipate another memorable event that will bring to our lives more wonderful memories to cherish for years to come! With the familiar, tempting aromas and sounds emanating from the kitchen, even the "little ones" want to participate in the fun of holiday baking and making the holidays memorable. Encourage them and include them during preparations to make your holidays ones they will long remember and perhaps start some traditions that can be passed along to your children and grandchildren.

Today we live our lives at a hectic pace. However, even with all of the hustle and bustle, we can still build our own cherished family traditions. I'm excited to finally be able to share with you *Hallelujah Holidays,* an answer to my and your prayers! Use the recipes in this book to give you a starting place, then add some of your own ideas and traditions to help you fill your holidays with special joy and memories for you, your family, and friends!

May Our Heavenly Father richly bless you as you seek to make your holidays memorable and may He give you wisdom to make healthy choices so that you may offer Him your best for His service!

The Five-Star System

As stated earlier, my goal is to set before you healthier recipes for the holidays that complement the Hallelujah Diet and Lifestyle℠. To assist you in attaining that goal, you will find the five-star system throughout this recipe book. The following key should assist you in understanding this system and in working toward a goal of healthier holiday meals for you and your family.

Recipes with five stars are all raw and properly combined. These five-star recipes are foods that have been shown to have a profound health-producing effect on people who consume them on a regular basis. These foods should be consumed daily. It is these foods that provide the nutrients to strengthen our immune systems, which help to prevent or heal disease. Our bodies were designed by God to be self-healing, and these five-star recipes are properly and deliciously combined foods, containing nutrients in their simplest, raw form—as God created them—that help this self-healing to work. *Also please see note for those who have chronic degenerative conditions at the end of this section.*

Recipes with four stars are all raw but not properly combined. These are still excellent recipes, but should not be consumed as frequently as the five-star recipes because the ingredients used in four-star recipes do not digest as well together.

Recipes with three stars are the cooked, but properly combined recipes. They can be consumed every day as part of the 15 percent cooked portion of the evening meal.

Recipes with two stars are cooked, but not properly combined recipes or may be recipes with ingredients that should be consumed less frequently than the three-star recipes for that 15 percent cooked food portion of the evening meal.

★

Recipes with only one star are raw or cooked recipes with ingredients that should be used sparingly, for special occasions. They may include ingredients such as unbleached white flour, tofu, TVP, mustard, honey, maple syrup, date sugar, sucanat, vinegars other than the raw unfiltered apple cider vinegar, Vegenaise®, non-dairy milk or cheese. If you have serious health challenges, the one-star recipes should be omitted from the diet even if they are all raw because they are too high in protein or fat.

An example of a recipe that would earn no stars—and would not even be included in this book—is one that includes substances that have been shown to cause disease, such as meat (including fish and chicken), dairy, eggs, sugar, table salt, or chemical preservatives.

Note: We use a "five-star" rating system to help you determine the recipes that are most appropriate for your dietary and lifestyle goals. While even our "five-star" recipes are all raw and properly combined, we would encourage anyone dealing with chronic degenerative conditions such as cancer and heart disease to carefully consider eliminating or minimizing the use of raw nuts, seeds, and most unrefined oils with the exception of either flaxseed oil or Udo's oil (if dealing with prostate cancer, freshly ground flaxseed may be a better option than either of these oils).

The Hallelujah Diet

Breakfast: Upon rising, take one serving of BarleyMax®, either in capsule or powder form. (Take the powder dry, dissolving it in the mouth, or mix it in a few ounces of distilled water at room temperature.) Do not eat cooked food, or foods containing fiber at this meal, as these hinder the cleansing process while the body eliminates accumulated toxins.

Mid-Morning: Drink an eight-ounce glass of fresh vegetable juice (2/3 carrot and 1/3 greens). If fresh juice is not available, the next best choice is a combination serving of CarrotJuiceMax™ and BarleyMax®, or a piece of juicy, fresh fruit.

Lunch: Before lunch, have another serving of BarleyMax®, taken as at breakfast. Thirty minutes later, eat either a raw vegetable salad or raw fruit. This also is an all-raw meal, as cooked food is limited to the evening meal. Fruit should be limited to no more than 15% of total daily food intake.

Mid-Afternoon: Drink an eight-ounce glass of carrot/vegetable juice. If juice is not available, a serving of CarrotJuiceMax™, BeetMax, or some carrot or celery sticks are second best.

Supper: Before dinner, have another serving of BarleyMax®, taken as at breakfast and lunch. Thirty minutes later, eat a LARGE green salad comprised of leaf lettuce (never head lettuce as it has very little nutritional value) along with a variety of vegetables. After the salad comes the only cooked food of the day the 15% cooked food portion allowed on The Hallelujah Diet®. This could be a baked potato, brown rice, steamed veggies, whole grain pasta, or a veggie sandwich on whole grain bread, baked sweet potato, or squash. (If desired, Lunch and Supper can be switched, but only one meal should contain cooked food on any given day.)

Evening: If desired, a piece of juicy, fresh fruit or a glass of freshly extracted apple or pear juice may be consumed.

The Hallelujah Diet Explained

The Hallelujah Diet®, once understood, is very simple. We follow a ratio of 85% raw and 15% cooked food each day, with the cooked food usually coming only at the end of the evening meal.

The 85% Portion

This is an abundance of God's natural foods, uncooked (raw), and unprocessed. The dense living nutrients found in raw foods and their juices are what meet and satisfy our cells nutritional needs, so that a person no longer needs to struggle with uncontrollable hunger. Live foods are also what produce abundant energy and vibrant health. The following are items from each category that fit into the 85% portion of each day's food intake:

Beverages: Freshly extracted vegetable juices, BarleyMax®, CarrotJuiceMax™, BeetMax, and distilled water.

Dairy Alternatives: Fresh almond milk, creamy banana milk, as well as frozen banana, strawberry, or blueberry fruit creams.

Fruit: All fresh, as well as unsulphured organic dried fruit. Limited to no more than 15% of daily food intake.

Grains: Soaked oats, millet, raw muesli, dehydrated granola, dehydrated cracker.

Beans: Green beans, peas, sprouted garbonzo, sprouted lentils, and sprouted mung.

Nuts and Seeds: Raw almonds, sunflower seeds, macadamia nuts, walnuts, raw almond butter or tahini, and raw ground flaxseed. Consume sparingly.

Oils and Fats: Extra virgin olive oil, Udo's Choice Perfected Oil Blend™, flaxseed oil (the oil of choice for people with cancer, except men with prostate cancer, who may be better served meeting the essential fat needs through freshly ground flaxseed), and avocados.

Seasonings: Fresh or dehydrated herbs, garlic, sweet onions, parsley, and salt-free seasonings.

Soups: Raw soups.

Sweets: Fruit smoothies, raw fruit pies with nut/date crusts, date-nut squares, etc.

Vegetables: All raw vegetables.

The 15% Portion

The following foods make up the 15% portion of The Hallelujah Diet®. These cooked foods follow the raw salad at the evening meal. This cooked food portion can be very delicious, and actually proves beneficial for those trying to maintain body weight.

Beverages: Caffeine-free herb teas and cereal-based coffee-like beverages, along with bottled organic juices.

Beans: Lima, adzuki, black, kidney, navy, pinto, red, and white.

Dairy: Non-dairy cheese, rice milk, and organic butter. (Use sparingly.)

Fruit: Stewed and unsweetened frozen fruits.

Grains: Whole-grain cereals, breads, muffins, pasta, brown rice, millet, etc.

Oils: Mayonnaise made from cold-pressed oils.

Seasonings: Same as 85% portion, plus unrefined Sea Salt (Use sparingly.)

Soups: Soups made from scratch without fat, dairy, or table salt.

Sweeteners: Raw, unfiltered honey, rice syrup, unsulphured molasses, stevia, carob, pure maple syrup, date sugar. (Use very sparingly.)

Vegetables: Steamed or wok-cooked fresh or frozen vegetables, baked white or sweet potatoes, squash, etc.

While this list at first appears limiting, there are hundreds, if not thousands, of exciting recipes that meet these criteria. See our selection of recipe books for additional ideas.

Foods to Avoid

These foods create most of the physical problems we experience, and are NOT a part of The Hallelujah Diet®. They should be eliminated from the diet as quickly as possible.

Beverages: Alcohol, coffee, tea, cocoa, carbonated beverages and soft drinks, all artificial fruit drinks, including sports drinks, and all commercial juices containing preservatives, refined salt, and sweeteners.

Dairy: All milk, cheese, eggs, ice cream, whipped toppings, and non-dairy creamers.

Fruit: Canned and sweetened fruits, along with non-organic dried fruits.

Grains: Refined, bleached flour products, cold breakfast cereals, and white rice.

Meats: Beef, pork, fish, chicken, turkey, hamburgers, hot dogs, bacon, sausage, etc. All meats are harmful to the body and a contributing cause of most physical problems.

Nuts & Seeds: All roasted and/or salted seeds and nuts. Peanuts are not a nut but a legume, and very difficult to digest.

Oils: All lard, margarine, and shortenings. Anything containing hydrogenated oils.

Seasonings: Refined table salt, black pepper, and any seasonings containing them.

Soups: All canned, packaged, or creamed soups containing dairy products.

Sweets: All refined white or brown sugar, sugar syrups, chocolate, candy, gum, cookies, donuts, cakes, pies, or other products containing refined sugars or artificial sweeteners.

Vegetables: All canned vegetables with added preservatives, or vegetables fried in oil.

By Way Of Clarification

A Word About Mushrooms

Over the years we have been asked about mushrooms and whether they should be eaten since they are a fungus. The following are two opinions about them. Only you can decide if you wish to include mushrooms in your diet.

David Wolfe, author of *The Sunfood Diet Success System*, states on page 68: "Mushrooms: Not a true plant food, this fungus grows in darkness, and is not directly nourished by the vibrant Sun energy." And on page 186, he says: "Mushrooms are protein-dominant, but are not very concentrated, thus they create few obstructions. Mushrooms are a fungus, not a true Sunfood. They should be eaten in moderation."

Joel Fuhrman, author of *Eat to Live*, states on page 184: "Eat lots of mushrooms all the time…. Even though they are a fungus, and not a real vegetable, mushrooms contain a variety of powerful phytochemicals and have been linked to decreased risk of chronic diseases, especially cancer."

In this book, we have included mushrooms; however, it is your choice whether to use them or not.

A Word About Stevia

Scientific Name: Asteraceae
Common Name: Stevia

Historical Use: Stevia is derived from the leaf of an herb that was discovered in Paraguay in 1887. During WWII Stevia was used as a sweetener in England when sugarcane supplies were unavailable. Over the years, it has also been used in South America, Taiwan, China, Malaysia, South Korea and in Japan since about 1970.

Common Use: Stevia is used as a sweetener in beverages and foods. A study in Japan (Isima 1976) found that Stevia is approximately 300 times sweeter than table sugar so only a small amount is required to sweeten beverages and foods. Therefore, Stevia is considered to add very few calories but as with all sweeteners, Stevia should be used in moderation.

Investigative Reports: Ray Sahelian, M. D. and Donna Gates report in, *The Stevia Cookbook,* that some studies indicate that Stevia may contribute to the lowering of blood cholesterol, blood sugar, tooth decay and weight loss.

Forms Available: Although Stevia is available in capsule form or as dried leaves, the most common way it is found is in a powder or liquid form.

Usage: As a sweetener in recipes:

Stevia Conversions:		
Sugar Amount	Equivalent Stevia Powder	Equivalent Stevia Liquid
1 cup	1 tsp.	1 tsp.
1 Tbsp.	¼ tsp.	6 to 9 drops
1 tsp.	A pinch (¹⁄₁₆ to ⅛ tsp.)	2 to 4 drops
If using the liquid form, 1–2 drops may be all that is needed to sweeten tea. The amount may be increased depending upon the level of sweetness desired.		

Taste: Although very sweet, some have noted that Stevia can have a bit of an aftertaste.

For more information: Read *The Stevia Cookbook* available from Hallelujah Acres.

Steam Sauté Versus Oil Sauté

At Hallelujah Acres® we steam sauté or dry roast rather than using oil to sautéing because all heated oils are potentially harmful to the body. Therefore, any recipe that calls for sautés in oil is given a one-star (★) rating. Many of these same recipes would be a three-star (★★★) if the recipes were changed and steam sautéing were used instead. Be aware that changing the recipe will alter the flavor somewhat but the health advantages are out of this world. The choice is yours!

Soaking Nuts And Seeds

You will find that nuts and seeds used in this book are soaked and drained before using. All nuts and seeds contain growth inhibitors that prevent the seed or nut from sprouting too early if they are exposed to a small amount of moisture. Charlotte Gerson*, founder of the Gerson Institute, advises that these growth inhibitors become cell inhibitors within the human body. However, once the seed or nut has begun to sprout, the cell inhibitors are rendered harmless as the seed or nut begins to break down. At this time, the body can easily absorb the nutrients that the seeds and nuts contain.

*Note: Charlotte Gerson is the daughter of Dr. Max Gerson, one of the early pioneers of nutrition-based, non-toxic therapy. As a young medical student, he suffered from incapacitating migraine headaches. He was told they were incurable and that he would have to learn to live with them. Looking for relief from the debilitating headaches, which kept him in bed for days, he began to examine what he ate. He discovered that by restricting his diet and avoiding salt, fats, pickled and smoked food, and by eating fresh fruits and vegetables he could control his headaches. From that time on he dedicated his life to researching the relationship between diet and disease. One of his patients was Dr. Albert Schweitzer's wife, Helena. Dr. Albert Schweitzer said of Dr. Max Gerson, "I see in Dr. Max Gerson one of the eminent geniuses in medical history." At that time, The Gerson Diet became revolutionary in the treatment of cancer. Based on the vision, philosophy, and research of her father, Charlotte Gerson founded The Gerson Institute in 1977. The Gerson Institute, which is located in Tijuana, Mexico, continues to this day.

At Hallelujah Acres we recommend soaking nuts and seeds. Soaking allows the enzyme inhibitors to be dissipated and makes them easier for the body to digest and utilize. The following chart is a guide to assist you in your kitchen endeavors.

Nuts	Soaking Time
Almonds	8–12 hours
Brazil Nuts	8–12 hours
Macadamia Nuts	5–7 hours
Pecans	2–4 hours
Pine Nuts	1 hour
Pistachios	6–8 hours
Walnuts	8–10 hours
All other nuts	6 hours

Seeds	Soaking Time
Flax Seeds	½–1 hour
Sunflower Seeds, hulled	6–8 hours
Pumpkin Seeds	6–12 hours
Sesame Seeds	6–8 hours

Note: Most hard nuts and seeds can be soaked overnight while softer nuts take only a few hours. Once the nuts or seeds have been soaked, they may be dehydrated at 105 degrees until thoroughly dry and then stored in the refrigerator or freezer until needed.

Dried Fruits
1–2 hours in enough distilled water to cover*

*If soaking large amounts of fruit, allow more time and use the following measurements: 1 cup fruit to 2 cups liquid, cover and soak in the refrigerator several hours or overnight.

Non-Dairy Butter, Sour Cream, Etc.

When you find these terms, please do not even consider soy products as an alternative. Soy is not an option on The Hallelujah Diet® as it is too high in protein and very difficult for the body to digest and assimilate. Use rice milk, rice butter, or the Sunflower Sour Cream recipe found in this book.

How To Use The Recipes In This Book

Many people on The Hallelujah Diet® find the diet is not difficult to follow most days of the year. However, when it comes to the holidays, they often don't know what foods they can prepare that are in keeping with the holiday, while still being healthy and tasty. The recipes in this book are designed to help such people prepare a special meal.

This book contains 300 recipes that are designed to help you serve anything from a casual holiday meal to a full seven-course holiday banquet. The book is divided into eight sections: (1) Beverages, (2) Sauces, Dips, Relishes, and Spreads, (3) Soups, Stews, and Chowders, (4) Salads, (5) Dressings, (6) Entrees, (7) Breads, and (8) Desserts. In it you will also find ideas for Gifts to Share, How to use Fresh Herbs, How to Prepare for a Holiday Dinner Party, many

Helpful Kitchen Tips, and much more. In each chapter, there are numerous recipes from which to choose.

The first decision you will need to make is whether you wish to serve an all-raw dinner or one that includes some cooked items. If you're seeking to serve an all-raw dinner, look for the four-star and five-star recipes. If you are looking for a cooked recipe, then the three-star recipes would be the best. The two-star and one-star recipes are included to add variety and may be used for special occasions.

1. Choose a fresh juice from pages 23 to 35 or make your favorite. As your guests arrive you might offer them a fresh juice from your kitchen. Just go through the juice chapter and find a juice to your liking, prepare it, and serve it to your guests. If the affair is formal, serve the juice in stemmed glasses. Juice made from carrot and beet is very festive in appearance. You may also wish to have available another beverage for those guests who may not care for juice but may enjoy Roma, Wassail, spiced cider, punch, etc.

2. Have several dips and sauces available for your guests to enjoy with fresh vegetables, dehydrated crackers, or fruit. You will find many Dips, Sauces, and Spreads in the chapter with the same name to give you lots of choices to make your dinner memorable. See pages 37 to 56.

3. Select a salad or two making sure they are colorful and fresh to serve your guests along with two or three dressings you've made. For salad recipes see pages 79 to 108 and for dressing recipes see pages 111 to 119.

4. Look through the Soup, Stews, and Chowders recipes on pages 59 to 76 to see if you can find a recipe for your special holiday meal. Bear in mind, the soup can be either raw or cooked and you don't have to serve large bowls, small bowls are rather nice or a cup of soup would be delightful.

5. Select one or two of the many bread recipes from raw to baked to have available to serve your guests. See pages 165 to 193. Serve the bread with your meal along with a spread, if you so desire. Notice that both raw and cooked breads have been included so you have a wide variety to choose from.

6. Next would come the Entrée part of the meal. You could select a recipe or two, either raw or cooked to suit your taste buds and those of your guests on pages 121 to 163. Perhaps you have your own favorite or a family recipe you'd like to consider using or upgrading to fit the Hallelujah Diet®.

7. Dessert may also be served, if desired, and there are many to choose from. Look on pages 195 to 229 to find one that will tantalize your taste buds and leave those who came to your house for dinner with wonderful memories to cherish of that special dinner.

To aid in holiday planning of special meals, included is a special section in the back of this book entitled: *How to Plan a Holiday Dinner Party*. It gives step-by-step directions so that any party can be a holiday to remember.

Don't forget to plan ahead so that you can find some time to relax and enjoy the time with those you love.

Beverages

*"Whether therefore ye eat, or drink, or whatsoever ye do,
do all to the glory of God."*

—*1 Corinthians 10:31*

*My childhood memories are precious thanks to my parents. They made
every holiday special, instilling in me the love for the season, good food
and spending time with loved ones.*

Carrot juice is the number one juice in George's and my diet. It is so nutrient dense including abundant amounts of vitamins B, C, D, E, K, and beta-carotene, a precursor of vitamin A, as well as calcium, phosphorous, potassium, sodium, and many other minerals and trace minerals. Carrot juice also contains calcium and magnesium, which helps to maintain the intestinal walls and helps to strengthen the bones and teeth. Carrot juice acts as a cleanser for the liver, explaining why we sometimes get a little orange tint in the palms of our hands when first starting to consume carrot juice. The body is simply releasing toxins from the liver to be removed from the body. Contrary to popular opinion, turning orange is not a sign of too much vitamin A. The pro-vitamin A (beta-carotene) in carrot juice is converted to vitamin A within the body. If you feel your skin is turning too orange, simply cut back a little on your juice consumption or dilute the carrot juice slightly with other vegetable juices, an apple, or distilled water. Another advantage of consuming carrot juice on a regular basis is the liver is able to release stale bile and excess fat, which contribute to high cholesterol.

Note: In preparation for juicing, we recommend that carrots be peeled (the juice is sweeter); also remove both top and bottom tips. Toxic chemical sprays are usually used in the growing of commercial produce; therefore, we at Hallelujah Acres strongly recommend that all non-organic vegetables and fruits with skins be peeled before consumption. We also recommend that all fresh fruits and vegetables that cannot be peeled should be washed with a vegetable and fruit wash, and dried, before consumption—even if they are organic.

Additionally, remember to have the screen in place and a catch container under the machine each time you juice.

CARROT JUICE

1 pound of carrots = 8 ounces of carrot juice

With machine running, process carrots through juicer.

FRESH FROM THE GARDEN JUICE

★★★★★	Serves 1
4–6	carrots
½	small cucumber, peeled
1	celery rib (stalk), washed and cut into chunks
½	beet with greens

With machine running, process carrots, cucumber, celery, and beet through juicer alternating ingredients.

SWEET DELIGHT

★★★★★	Serves 1
4–6	carrots
1	hard red apple, quartered
1	celery rib (stalk), cut in large chunks

With machine running, process apple, celery, and carrots alternately through juicer.

BLUSHING APPLE JUICE

★★★★★	Serves 1
2	sweet apples (Gala, Golden Delicious, or other sweet apple)
¼	beet
¼	lemon including rind (if organic)

Cut apples and beets into pieces and juice along with ¼ of the lemon..

POPEYE SPINACH JUICE

★★★★★	Serves 1
4–6	carrots
Handful	Spinach
1	sweet apple (Gala, Golden Delicious, or other sweet apple)
1	celery rib (stalk), cut into chunks

Prepare ingredients, cut apple just prior to using and celery into chunks before processing juice.

HOLIDAY JUICE
Deborah Martin

★★★★★	Serves 24–30
12 medium	carrots
40	hard red apples
6 medium	beets

Juice apples, carrots and beets; blend together, serve immediately.

BONE BUILDING JUICE

★★★★★	Serves 1
4–6	carrots
3	kale leaves
2	sprigs of parsley
½	sweet apple

Wash greens. Cut apple into quarters and juice all ingredients.

BLUSHING CARROT JUICE

★★★★★	Serves 1
4–5	carrots
½	beet with greens

Cut beet into wedges and alternate it through the juicer with the carrots.

KNOCK YOUR SOCKS OFF JUICE

★★★★★	Serves 1
5	carrots
½	sweet red apple
¼-inch piece	gingerroot
3 or 4 sprigs	parsley

Cut apple in wedges and feed through the juicer with the gingerroot, parsley, and carrots.

GREEN POWER JUICE

★★★★★	Serves 1
4–5	carrots
1–2	celery ribs (stalks)
Handful	dark leafy greens
1–3 sprigs	parsley

Run ingredients through juicer alternating carrots with greens.

LOVE THAT GARLIC JUICE

★★★★★	Serves 1
6	carrots
2	celery ribs (stalks)
Handful	spinach
2 cloves	garlic, peeled

Cut celery in chunks and feed through juicer with spinach and garlic alternating with carrots.

BELL PEPPER DELIGHT

★★★★★	Serves 1
4–6	carrots
½ large	red bell pepper, seeded
Handful	spinach
1–2 sprigs	parsley

Cut bell pepper into chunks and feed bell pepper, spinach, and parsley alternately with carrots.

SUNRISE SURPRISE

★★★★★	Serves 1
5–6	carrots
1	sweet apple
½	beet with greens
¼-inch piece	gingerroot (or to taste)

Cut apple and beets in chunks and feed all ingredients through the juicer alternating with the carrots.

SALAD IN A GLASS

★★★★★	Serves 1
4–6	carrots
Handful	broccoli florets
½	cucumber
1	celery rib (stalk)

Peel cucumber, as the skin can be bitter. Cut the celery into chunks and run the vegetables through the juicer alternating with the carrots*.

Option: Add other vegetables as desired.

***Rhonda's Kitchen Tips:** More juice recipes can be found in *Recipes for Life … from God's Garden.*

HOT CAROB WHIP

★	Serves 2
2½ cups	distilled water
2 tsp.	Roma (or other coffee substitute available in Health Food Stores)
1 tbsp.	carob powder (available in Health Food Stores)
¼ cup	non-dairy milk powder
2 tsp.	sweetener (2–3 pitted dates, raw unfiltered honey, or maple syrup)
1 tsp.	pure vanilla (optional)

Place all ingredients in a blender to mix well. May serve cold or pour blended ingredients into a saucepan and heat to desired temperature. Do not boil.

WASSAIL
Greg Tabor

★★★	Serves 9–10
4 cups	organic apple juice
3 cups	unsweetened pineapple juice
2 cups	organic cranberry juice
¼ tsp.	ground nutmeg
2	cinnamon sticks
5	whole cloves
5	lemon slices

Combine ingredients in a large pan and simmer for 10 minutes. Strain and serve hot.

SPICED CIDER

★★★	Serves 8
2–3	3-inch cinnamon sticks
1 tbsp.	allspice berries
1 tbsp.	whole cloves
4 tsp.	coarsely grated orange rind (zest)
1	sweet apple, cored and sliced into rings
1	organic gallon apple cider
5	lemon slices

Place cinnamon sticks, allspice berries and whole cloves into a 6-inch square cheesecloth, bring up corners and tie securely with a string. Combine remaining ingredients and spice bag in a large saucepan or slow cooker and simmer over low heat at least 2 hours to allow flavors to mingle. Remove spice bag, oranges, lemons and apples before serving.

Note: May replace 4 teaspoons coarsely grated orange rind placed in cheesecloth with one organic thinly sliced orange placed in cider.

HOLIDAY SHAKE

★★★★	Serves 1
8 ounces	distilled water
2 tbsp.	non-dairy milk
2 large	dates, pitted
1	ripe banana
2 tsp.	whole flaxseeds (ground if not using a Vita-Mix)
Dash	cinnamon and nutmeg (optional)

Place all ingredients in Vita-Mix or blender and process until creamy.

CINNAMON TEA
Karen Risk

★★★

Boil some cinnamon sticks in distilled water to make your own cinnamon tea. The tea is naturally sweet, and very good. That's it.

HOLIDAY "EGGNOG"

★★★★★	Serves 4
2 cups	almond milk (see recipe on page 35.)
2	medium ripe bananas, peeled
¼	tsp. pure vanilla
Dash	nutmeg

Combine first three ingredients in blender. Blend until smooth. Serve immediately with a dash of nutmeg on top.

HOLIDAY NOG
Shari Viger

★★★★★	Serves 4
1 quart	of your favorite almond milk (see recipe on page 35.)
2 tsp.	whole cardamom
2 tsp.	broken cinnamon sticks
2 tsp.	fennel seeds
2 tsp.	whole cloves
2 tsp.	fresh ground nutmeg

Put all of the spices in a clean coffee grinder and grind until fine. (If you don't have whole cardamom, cinnamon sticks, fennel seeds, or whole cloves, you can substitute with ground spices.) Add 2 tsp. of the spice mixture to a quart of your favorite almond milk recipe. Blend very well in your blender, pour and serve immediately. Store left over spices in a dark glass container with a tight lid.

HOT CRANBERRY PUNCH

★	Yield: about 3 quarts
6 cups	organic fruit sweetened cranberry juice
4 cups	fresh orange juice
6 ounces	fresh lemon juice
1 cup	distilled water
¼ cup	date sugar or to taste
3 tsp.	whole cloves
3 tsp.	ground allspice
1	whole nutmeg, crushed
5	3-inch cinnamon sticks, broken into pieces

Combine first five ingredients and place in large saucepan. Wrap spices in cheesecloth and tie securely. Add to saucepan. Bring mixture to a boil, stirring occasionally. Reduce heat to low, cover and simmer for 30 minutes. Remove spice bag and serve hot.

CRANBERRY AND APPLE PUNCH
Deborah Martin

★★★★★	Serves 25
10 lbs.	apples
2-8 oz. pks.	cranberries
20	pears
1 cup	fresh cranberries for ice mold

Juice and blend apple, cranberry, and pear juices.

To make ice ring, place cranberries in a mold with some of the mixed juices and freeze. Serve in punch bowl with ice ring.

ALMOST BUTTERMILK

★	1 cup
1–2 tbsp.	lemon juice or raw unfiltered apple cider vinegar
1 cup	non-dairy milk

Combine ingredients and mix well with wire whip. Set aside for 5 minutes to "work" before serving or using in a recipe.

LEMONADE

★★★★★	Serves 8–10
10–12	Golden Delicious apples, washed, cored and cut into large pieces
1 large	organic lemon or 2 small, washed unpeeled and quartered

Process the lemons through the juicer followed by the apples. (This helps the lemonade not to brown as quickly). The more yellow the apples the prettier the lemonade. Other apples may be used, but for the best flavor use Yellow Delicious and serve immediately over ice.

BENJAMIN'S LEMONADE
Suzy and Michael Horseus

★★★★★
Lemons
Stevia
Distilled water

My 8-year-old son loves this simple drink. We mix the juice and pulp of lemons (oranges and grapefruit depending upon our supply), a few drops of stevia (sweetened to taste), and distilled water.

IN THE PINK SHAKE

★★★★	Serves 1
2 ounces	organic cranberry juice
4 ounces	fresh organic orange juice
1	tangerine or ½ orange, peeled and quartered
¼ cup	fresh or frozen cranberries
1	ripe banana

Place all ingredients in Vita-Mix or blender and process until creamy.

FRUIT SMOOTHIE

★★★★★	
2 or 3	bananas, peeled and frozen
½ cup	organic apple juice

Place ingredients in a blender and blend until creamy. Additional apple juice may be added if needed.

Option: Add any fruit that is in season or that you have frozen. If adding fresh fruit, the smoothie will not be as thick as when using frozen.

SWEET ALMOND MILK

★★★★★	Serves 2
½ cup	raw almonds, soaked overnight and drained
2–3	Medjool Dates, pitted, soaked overnight in 2 cups distilled water (save soaking water)
¼ cup	unsweetened coconut
1	vanilla bean, ground or ¾ tsp. pure vanilla
½ tsp.	cinnamon (optional)

Place dates in a jar with 2 cups of distilled water, cover, and place in the refrigerator overnight. The following morning, place almonds along with dates, soaking water, unsweetened coconut, and spices in a blender or Vita-Mix and process until creamy. If not using a Vita-Mix, before serving, strain "milk" through cheesecloth or fine strainer to remove any remaining pulp. Will keep 2–3 days in the refrigerator.

PLAIN ALMOND MILK

★★★★★	Serves 2
½ cup	raw almonds, soaked overnight and drained
2 cups	distilled water

Place almonds and distilled water in a blender or Vita-Mix and process until creamy. This may be used in any recipe that calls for milk. Strain through fine strainer if not using a Vita-Mix.

ALMOND BUTTER SMOOTHIE
Marjorie Dockery

★	Serves 1
1–2	frozen bananas (peeled and sliced before freezing)
1 tbsp.	raw almond butter
1 cup	rice milk or other non-dairy milk
2 tbsp.	fresh ground flaxseed

Put all ingredients in Vita-Mix or blender and process until creamy, adding more rice milk as needed to reach desired consistency.

Sauces, Dips, Relishes, and Spreads

"Who satisfieth thy mouth with good things; so that thy youth is renewed like the eagle's!"

—*Psalm 103:5*

A house symbolizes so much: a safe haven, roots, security. But it takes real family to make a house a home. My grandfather built our simple house in March 1931, during the depression, for only $5000, and to me, it was the world! I have so many warm memories of our entire family gathered here for the holidays.

RAW CRANBERRY SAUCE

★	Serves 6–8
2 cups	fresh cranberries, ground*
1	orange (washed to remove any residues) chop very fine including at least ½ of the rind
2	ripe pears, peeled and chopped fine
1 medium	apple, peeled and chopped fine
½ cup	walnuts or pecans, chopped into pieces
4	celery ribs (stalks), chopped fine
½ cup	organic raisins or dates (pit and chop dates if using)
½–1 tsp.	cinnamon or pumpkin pie spice
¼ tsp.	ginger
¼ tsp.	allspice
½ cup	raw, unfiltered honey or other sweetener**

Grind berries, chop fruit, mince nuts, chop celery and dates if using. Place all ingredients in a bowl and mix well. Cover and place in the refrigerator until ready to serve. Serve on a bed of leaf lettuce.

*Option: Leave cranberries whole and place in a saucepan with all remaining ingredients. Turn burner to low and simmer until thickened, stirring occasionally.

**Option: Replace ½ cup honey or other sweetener with ½ cup soaked, pitted and pureed dates and this becomes a four-star (★★★★) recipe.

RAW ITALIAN SAUCE

★★★★★	Serves 8

To make the sauce:

1 cup	fresh carrot juice
1 large	tomato or 2 cups cherry tomatoes
½ cup	dehydrated tomato flakes (optional)
2	Medjool dates, pitted, soaked one hour and drained
1	celery rib (stalk), cut in 1-inch chunks
½ large	sweet onion, cut in pieces
½ cup	pine nuts*, soaked 6–8 hours and drained
1	red sweet bell pepper, seeded
2 cloves	garlic, peeled
½ cup	fresh basil
¼ cup	fresh oregano
	Celtic Sea Salt® to taste (optional)
¼ cup	extra virgin cold pressed olive oil (optional)

Place above 13 ingredients in blender or Vita-Mix and process until smooth. If using Vita-Mix, turn on the machine and use tamper to push vegetables into the blades. If not, stop machine frequently and push vegetables into blades and process until creamy. Pour pureed sauce into a bowl and add the following chopped vegetables, if desired.

Finely chop the following vegetables:

½	tomato or ¾ cup cherry tomatoes
1	celery rib (stalk)
1 bunch	scallions
½	red bell pepper, seeded
1 large	carrot

*__Rhonda's Kitchen Tips:__ Pine nuts (pignoli or pignolia) are the edible, soft, white seed of a number of western North American pine trees. They add versatility in the kitchen with a creamy consistency when used in sauces or dressings and a wonderful texture when used whole. Because pine nuts have a very short shelf life, they should be stored in the freezer.

SWEET AND SOUR SAUCE

★	Yield: Approximately 1¼ cups
½ cup	organic orange juice
½ cup	fresh lemon juice
½ cup	Medjool dates, pitted and soaked in enough distilled water to cover for 2 hours
½ cup	dried apricots, soaked in enough distilled water to cover for 2 hours
½ cup	pineapple pieces
¼–½-inch	piece of fresh ginger
¼ tsp.	ground mustard
1 tbsp.	extra virgin cold pressed olive oil
½ tsp.	Celtic Sea Salt® (optional)

Drain dates and apricots. Place all ingredients in Vita-Mix, blender, or food processor with an "S" blade and blend until desired consistency. Keeps several days in a sealed jar in the refrigerator.

SWEET MANGO SAUCE
Joyce Welsh

★★★★★	Serves 2
1	mango, peeled and seeded

Put all of the fruit including the juice (but not the seed) in a blender or Vita-Mix. Blend until smooth. Use as a sauce for any combination of cut up fruit. For instance, take a cup of strawberries or watermelon or cantaloupe or any combination of raw fruit cleaned and cut up and then pour the mango over the top.

Or cut a cantaloupe in half, take out the seeds, and then fill the hole with the blended mango.

This simple mango treat is pretty and sweet enough to serve at a dinner party and so easy to make.

BARBECUE SAUCE

★★★★	Yield: Approximately 3 cups
2–3 cloves	garlic, peeled
1 large	sweet onion, chopped
2	bell peppers, seeded and chopped
1 cup	tomato sauce or tomato puree
½ cup	dehydrated tomato flakes
6 large	dates, soaked in distilled water for 2 hours and drained
½ cup	extra virgin cold pressed olive oil
¼ cup	lemon juice
1 tbsp.	raw unfiltered apple cider vinegar
¼ tsp.	paprika
	Celtic Sea Salt® to taste (optional)

Place all ingredients in a blender and blend until smooth. Place in container and store in refrigerator.

or

★★★	

Slowly steam sauté garlic, onion, and peppers in their own juices. Add remaining ingredients except olive oil and simmer for 15–20 minutes on medium heat. Fold in olive oil after removing from heat source. Barbecue sauce stores well in a tightly sealed container up to one week in the refrigerator.

SWEET GREEN DIP SAUCE
Lena Buhr

★★★★	Yield: Approximately 1½ cups
1	ripe avocado, peeled and pitted
1	ripe banana, peeled and cut into chunks

Mix or blend until smooth, and there you have it! If you like, serve it with nice greens and cherry tomatoes, cut in half. I'm addicted to this very tasty dip and couldn't live without it! It's so smooth. This dip is perfect for small children!

ALLA CHECCA
(Classic Raw Tomato Sauce)
Donna J. Young

★★★★★	Yield: Approximately 3 cups
5	tomatoes, cored and diced
4 cloves	garlic, peeled and minced (or to taste)
½ cup	fresh basil, chopped
½ cup	extra virgin cold pressed olive oil
	Celtic Sea Salt® (optional)

Combine tomatoes, garlic, basil, and olive oil in medium bowl. Add sea salt to taste, cover with plastic wrap and set it on counter for at least 2 hours or as long as 10 hours. Pour over hot pasta and top with non-dairy Parmesan, if desired.

Makes enough for 1 pound of pasta.

McAFEE'S SPECIAL SAUCE
Catherine McAfee

★★★★★	Yield: Approximately ¾ cup

This is a sauce that I like to put on top of rice. It is also good with quinoa, potatoes, or used as a salad dressing.

1	sweet red bell pepper, seeded
2–4 cloves	garlic, peeled
1 tbsp.	pine nuts*
	Squeeze of lime juice
	Small amount of distilled water

Put all ingredients into a blender and blend until smooth.

Rhonda's Kitchen Tips: Pine nuts (pignoli or pignola) are the edible, soft, white seed of a number of western North American pine trees. They add versatility in the kitchen with a creamy consistency when used in sauces or dressings and a wonderful texture when used whole. Because pine nuts have a very short shelf life, they should be stored in the freezer.

PINE NUT "CHEESE" SAUCE

★	Yield: Approximately 2½ cups
1 cup	distilled water
1 cup	pine nuts*, soaked 2 hours and drained
1 small	sweet red pepper, seeded (about ¼–½ cup)
2 tbsp.	onion flakes (or 1 tsp. onion powder)
¼ cup	nutritional yeast flakes
1 tbsp.	non-dairy Parmesan cheese**
½ tsp.	Celtic Sea Salt®
2 tsp.	paprika
½ tsp.	garlic powder or ½ small garlic clove, peeled
2 tbsp.	arrowroot powder or potato flour
¼ cup	fresh lemon juice

Place pine nuts and water in a blender or Vita-Mix and process until smooth and creamy. Add remaining ingredients and process until a creamy texture is reached. Place in a small saucepan and simmer until thickened. Stir constantly. Remove from heat and place in a small container with lid. Store in refrigerator.

Rhonda's Kitchen Tips: Pine nuts (pignoli or pignolia) are the edible, soft, white seed of a number of western North American pine trees. They add versatility in the kitchen with a creamy consistency when used in sauces or dressings and a wonderful texture when used whole. Because pine nuts have a very short shelf life, they should be stored in the freezer.

**Option: Omit the non-dairy Parmesan cheese and this becomes a 3-star (★★★) recipe.

BASIC MARINADE

★★★★★	Yield: ¾ cup
½ cup	extra virgin cold pressed olive oil
4 cloves	garlic, peeled
	Juice of ½ lemon (I prefer Meyer Lemons)
2 tsp.	Italian Seasoning or herbs of choice
2 tsp.	dried basil
	Celtic Sea Salt® to taste (optional)

Place garlic in food processor with "S" blade and process until finely minced. Add remaining ingredients and pulse until well mixed. To make a sweeter marinade, add some soaked dates.

GUACAMOLE DIP

★★★★★	Yield: Approximately 2 cups
2	ripe avocados*, peeled and pitted
1	whole tomato or ½ cup dehydrated tomatoes
2–4	green onions or ¼ sweet red onion
1–2 cloves	garlic, peeled
	Juice of one lemon
	Celtic Sea Salt® to taste (optional)

Place all ingredients in a food processor using the "S" blade and process to desired consistency.

Rhonda's Kitchen Tips: Placing the pits back into the mixed guacamole will help to retard oxidization.

GUACAMOLE DIP FOR A PARTY

★★★★★	Serves 6–10
8–10	ripe avocados, peeled and pitted*
	Juice of 1–2 lemons
1	red bell pepper, seeded and diced
1	orange or yellow bell pepper, seeded and diced
¼ cup	fresh cilantro, chopped
1 bunch	scallions, chopped; mince white bulb
2–3 cloves	garlic, peeled and minced
	Cayenne pepper to taste (optional)
	Celtic Sea Salt® to taste (optional)

Place avocados and lemon juice in food processor with an "S" blade and process until creamy. Remove from processor bowl and fold in other ingredients. Serve with fresh vegetables or dehydrated crackers.

***Rhonda's Kitchen Tips:** Placing the pits back into the mixed guacamole will help to retard oxidization.

RANCH DIP

★	Yield: Approximately 1½ cups
1 cup	Vegenaise®
⅛ cup	extra virgin cold pressed olive oil
	Juice of 1 large lemon or 2 small lemons
1–2 tsp.	raw unfiltered apple cider vinegar
1 tsp.	raw unfiltered honey
2 tsp.	dill weed

Whisk all ingredients together and store in refrigerator.

Option: Try different spices to vary the taste; Oriental seasoning is tasty.

SPINACH DIP

Jackie Graff, R.N., B.S.N., Raw Foods Chef

★★★★★	Yield: 6 cups
2 cups	macadamia nuts, soaked for 8 hours and drained
2 cups	distilled water
2 tsp.	Celtic Sea Salt® (optional)
	Juice of 2 lemons
1 cup	pine nuts*, soaked for 8 hours and drained
2 tsp.	ground nutmeg
2 cloves	garlic, peeled and minced
3 cups	spinach, chopped fine
3	carrots, grated fine
1	sweet onion, chopped fine
2	celery ribs (stalks)

Place macadamia nuts, distilled water, sea salt, and lemon juice in Vita-Mix or blender and blend until smooth. Add pine nuts and blend until smooth. Place garlic in a food processor with the "S" blade and process well. Add spinach, carrots, celery, and onion, processing well. Place macadamia nut mixture in processor with vegetables, add nutmeg and more sea salt as desired and process well. Serve with chips or vegetables.

*__Rhonda's Kitchen Tips:__ Pine nuts (pignoli or pignolia) are the edible, soft, white seed of a number of western North American pine trees. They add versatility in the kitchen with a creamy consistency when used in sauces or dressings and a wonderful texture when used whole. Because pine nuts have a very short shelf life, they should be stored in the freezer.

DILL DIP

★	Yield: 3 Cups
1½ cups	non-dairy sour cream
1½ cups	Vegenaise®
2 tbsp.	fresh lemon juice
¼ cup	fresh parsley, minced
3 tbsp.	favorite herb seasoning
2 tbsp.	dill weed
2 tbsp.	onion, minced
Pinch	cayenne pepper (optional)
	Assorted fresh vegetables

Combine ingredients in a blender or Vita-Mix and process to blend well. Chill at least 3 hours to allow flavors to mingle. Serve with assorted vegetables for dipping.

Option: Cut top off of red and green bell peppers, remove and discard seeds and veins. Fill with dip and place on a serving platter with veggies for a festive look on your table.

SUNSNIP VEGGIE DIP
Judy Fleming, Hallelujah Acres Lifestyle Center,
Toronto Canada

★★★★★	Yield: Approximately 2¾ cups
1 cup	parsnips, diced
½ cup	sunflower seeds
1¼ cups	distilled water
2 tbsp.	fresh lemon juice

Blend all ingredients, place in bowl, and use for a dip for your favorite veggies!

Options: May add garlic, dill weed, minced onion, chives, or your favorite herbs to this dip to vary the flavor. May be used for a topping on baked potatoes.

PESTO VEGETABLE DIP

★	Yield: Approximately 3 cups
¾ cup	fresh parsley, chopped
¾ cup	fresh basil, chopped
¼ cup	pine nuts*, soaked one hour and drained
¼ cup	extra virgin cold pressed olive oil
1 clove	garlic, peeled
1 cup	Vegenaise®
1 cup	non-dairy sour cream
1 tsp.	salt-free seasoning
Pinch	cayenne pepper or to taste

Place parsley, basil, pine nuts, and olive oil in a blender or food processor (use "S" blade) and process until the mixture becomes a coarse meal. Add remaining ingredients and process until creamy.

*Rhonda's Kitchen Tips: Pine nuts (pignoli or pignolia) are the edible, soft, white seed of a number of western North American pine trees. They add versatility in the kitchen with a creamy consistency when used in sauces or dressings and a wonderful texture when used whole. Because pine nuts have a very short shelf life, they should be stored in the freezer.

BASIC PESTO SAUCE

★★★★★	Yield: Approximately 2¾ cups
2 cups	fresh basil leaves
⅓ cup	pine nuts*, soaked one hour and drained
1 large clove	garlic, minced or 2-3 small cloves
¼ cup	· extra virgin cold pressed olive oil or more, if needed
Pinch	Celtic Sea Salt® (optional)
Pinch	cayenne pepper (optional)

Rinse and pat dry basil leaves. Place in food processor with the "S" blade, Vita Mix or blender. Add garlic cloves and pine nuts. Blend to a creamy paste, add non-dairy Parmesan. If using a food processor, drizzle oil into chute while running. If not, transfer to a bowl and slowly add olive oil using a wooden spoon until well mixed.

GARLIC & ALMOND DIP

★	Yield: Approximately 3 cups
3 heads (about 25 cloves)	garlic, peeled
2 tbsp.	extra virgin cold pressed olive oil
2 tsp.	raw unfiltered apple cider vinegar
1 tsp.	vegetarian Worcestershire sauce
1 package	non-dairy cream cheese, softened
1 ½ cups	slivered almonds, toasted and finely chopped
1 cup	non-dairy sour cream
¼ cup	fresh parsley, chopped
¼ tsp.	dry mustard (optional)
½ tsp.	dried oregano leaves
½ tsp.	Celtic Sea Salt® (optional)

Preheat oven to 300 degrees. Place garlic and oil in a shallow baking dish, stirring until garlic is coated well. Bake 30 minutes or until golden brown. Drain garlic on paper towels and cool completely.

In food processor using "S" blade or in a blender place drained garlic, vinegar and Worcestershire sauce and process until garlic is finely chopped. Remove from bowl and set aside. Place cream cheese in processing bowl and process until smooth. Add garlic and remaining ingredients and process until thoroughly blended. Cover and refrigerate overnight. To serve bring to room temperature.

CRUNCHY CELERY RELISH

Donna J. Young

★	Yield: Approximately 6 cups
3 cups	celery, chopped
1 cup	green pepper, seeded and chopped
1 cup	red pepper, seeded and chopped
1 cup	organic Granny Smith apple, unpeeled and chopped
½ cup	red onion, chopped
1 clove	garlic, peeled and minced
½ cup	raw unfiltered apple cider vinegar (or lemon juice)
¼ cup	raw unfiltered honey
2 tbsp.	prepared mustard
½ tsp.	Celtic Sea Salt® (optional)
½ tsp.	celery seeds
½ tsp.	mustard seeds
¼ tsp.	cayenne pepper
¼ tsp.	ground allspice

Combine celery, green and red peppers, apple, onions, and garlic in a glass medium sized bowl and toss well to mix. Set aside. In a small saucepan, combine remaining ingredients and cook over medium heat for about 5 minutes or until heated through, whisking constantly. Pour over vegetable mixture, and stir to coat and mix. Spoon into glass jars, cool to room temperature. Chill 8 hours to allow flavors to blend. Store in refrigerator. This is a delicious relish.

SUNFLOWER SOUR CREAM

★★★★★	Yield: Approximately 1¾ cups
½ cup	raw sunflower seeds, soaked overnight and drained
½ cup	pine nuts*, soaked overnight and drained
½ cup	celery juice or distilled water
	Juice of 1 lemon
¼ cup	chopped sweet onion
½ tsp.	garlic powder
½ tsp.	Celtic Sea Salt® (optional)
1 tsp.	Udo's Oil or extra virgin cold pressed olive oil

Drain sunflower seeds and pine nuts, and discard soaking water. Place celery juice in blender and add the sunflower seeds and pine nuts and blend until smooth. Add lemon juice, onion, garlic, sea salt, and Udo's oil. Blend until smooth, adding enough water to achieve desired consistency. Refrigerate until needed. For a more authentic "sour cream" flavor, cover the container with cheesecloth and leave on the counter until slightly fermented. This will take from 4 to 8 hours, depending upon the temperature. Will store up to one week in a tight container in the refrigerator.

*__Rhonda's Kitchen Tips:__ Pine nuts (pignoli or pignolia) are the edible, soft, white seed of a number of western North American pine trees. They add versatility in the kitchen with a creamy consistency when used in sauces or dressings and a wonderful texture when used whole. Because pine nuts have a very short shelf life, they should be stored in the freezer.

GARLIC SPREAD

★★★★★	Yield: Approximately 2½ cups
2 cups	pine nuts*, soaked 8 hours and drained
2 tbsp.	extra virgin cold pressed olive oil
1 tbsp.	fresh lemon juice
2–3 cloves	garlic, peeled
¼ cup	fresh basil or thyme
¼ cup	fresh parsley, stemmed
	Pinch of cayenne pepper (optional)

Place all ingredients in a food processor with the "S" blade and process until creamy. Use on bread or raw crackers. Will keep about one week but the flavor will intensify over time.

Options: You can change the flavor of this spread by changing or omitting the herbs used. To have more of a butter flavor, add 1½ tsp. of butter flavoring.

*Rhonda's Kitchen Tips: Pine nuts (pignoli or pignolia) are the edible, soft, white seed of a number of western North American pine trees. They add versatility in the kitchen with a creamy consistency when used in sauces or dressings and a wonderful texture when used whole. Because pine nuts have a very short shelf life, they should be stored in the freezer.

EASY RAW HUMMUS
Deborah Martin

★★★★★	Yield: Approximately 6 cups
5 cups	zucchini, peeled and chopped
½ cup	raw tahini
4 cloves	garlic, peeled
½ cup	fresh lemon juice
¼ cup	extra virgin cold pressed olive oil
1½ tsp.	Celtic Sea Salt® (optional)
Pinch	cayenne pepper

Place all ingredients in a food processor and blend until smooth.

BLACK BEAN AND CORN SALSA

★★★	Yield: Approximately 5 cups
2 cups	black beans, cooked and drained
1½ cups	fresh sweet corn, cut from the cob
2 medium	tomatoes, diced
1 large	red bell pepper, seeded and diced
1 bunch	scallions, sliced
1	sweet onion, chopped
½ cup	fresh Cilantro, minced
¼ cup	fresh Italian Parsley, minced
⅓ cup	fresh lime or lemon juice
¼ cup	extra virgin cold pressed olive oil
1 tsp.	Celtic Sea Salt® (optional)
½ tsp.	dried cumin
Pinch	cayenne pepper (or to taste)

Combine all ingredients and mix well. Cover and place in the refrigerator for several hours to allow the flavors to blend.

ALMOND WHIPPING CREAM

★★★	Yield: 1 cup
2¾ cups	distilled water
1 tbsp.	arrowroot powder
1 tbsp.	oat flour
6–8	dates, chopped pitted and soaked 2 hours, or 2 tbsp. raw unfiltered honey
1 cup	almonds, soaked overnight and drained
1½ tsp.	pure vanilla
½ tsp.	Celtic Sea Salt® (optional)

Place ¾ cup distilled water and the above ingredients in a blender and process until smooth and creamy.

Bring the remaining 2 cups of distilled water to a boil; pour blender ingredients into boiling water while stirring constantly with wire whisk. Stir and cook until thickened nicely. Chill and serve as you would any other whipping cream.

PINE NUT CRÈME

★★★★★	Yield: Approximately 2½ cups
1 cup	pine nuts*, almonds, or macadamia nuts, soaked overnight and drained
1	Golden Delicious Apple
1 cup	distilled water

Place nuts in blender or food processor and slowly add water. Less water makes a thicker dressing so add the water slowly until desired consistency is reached.

For a festive color, blend in a couple of strawberries or ¼ cup raspberries or blueberries.

Put Fruit Salad into individual serving bowls and pour on the Pine Nut Crème. Garnish with small amount chopped nut pieces, if you wish.

Rhonda's Kitchen Tips: Pine nuts (pignoli or pignolia) are the edible, soft, white seed of a number of western North American pine trees. They add versatility in the kitchen with a creamy consistency when used in sauces or dressings and a wonderful texture when used whole. Because pine nuts have a very short shelf life, they should be stored in the freezer.

NOT BUTTERMILK

★	Yield: 1 cup
1–2 tbsp.	lemon juice or raw unfiltered apple cider vinegar
1 cup	non-dairy milk

Combine ingredients and mix well with a wire whip. Cover with plastic wrap and allow to set for 5 minutes.

MACADAMIA PINE NUT CHEESE

Jackie Graff, R.N., B.S.N., Raw Foods Chef

★★★★★	Yield: Approximately 5 cups
2 cups	macadamia nuts, soaked for 8 hours and drained
2 cups	distilled water
1 tsp.	Celtic Sea Salt® (optional)
¼ cup	fresh lemon juice
1 cup	pine nuts*, soaked for 8 hours and drained

Place macadamia nuts, distilled water, sea salt, and lemon juice in a Vita-Mix or blender and blend until smooth. Add pine nuts and blend again until smooth. At this point, this recipe can be used to replace yogurt in any recipe.

To ferment cheese, place in a dish in dehydrator and dehydrate for 8–12 hours until it resembles cream cheese or ricotta cheese. Stir several times during the dehydration process, as a crust will form on top.

This "cheese" may be used as Parmesan replacement by spreading about ¼ cup very thinly on a piece of parchment paper that has been placed on a dehydrator sheet. Dehydrate until thoroughly dry. Remove from sheet and process in food processor until desired consistency is reached.

Rhonda's Kitchen Tips: Pine nuts (pignoli or pignolia) are the edible, soft, white seed of a number of western North American pine trees. They add versatility in the kitchen with a creamy consistency when used in sauces or dressings and a wonderful texture when used whole. Because pine nuts have a very short shelf life, they should be stored in the freezer.

HEALTHY HEART BUTTER

Bev Cook, Hallelujah Acres Lifestyle Center℠

★★★	Yield: 1 pint

Start by making Cornmeal Mush:

Place the following ingredients in a saucepan, bring to a boil, and cook for 5 minutes, stirring constantly. Place lid on saucepan and remove from heat.

½ cup	cornmeal
1 cup	distilled water at room temperature

"Butter" Ingredients

¼ cup	distilled water
½ cup	raw almonds
1½ tsp.	butter flavoring
½ cup	coconut oil
¼ tsp.	Celtic Sea Salt® (optional)
⅓ cup	Thai coconut milk (or your favorite non-dairy milk)

Place the almonds and distilled water into a Vita-Mix or blender and process until creamy. Add the cornmeal mush along with the remaining ingredients except coconut milk. Blend until smooth adding coconut milk only if needed. Pour into small container, cover and store in refrigerator. Serve at room temperature.

This is an example of one of the recipes you will learn to prepare when you attend one of Bev and Chet Cook's retreats at the Hallelujah Acres Lifestyle Center℠ in Mill Spring, NC.

RHONDA'S MEXICAN SALSA

★★★★★	Yield: 2 Cups
6 medium	ripe tomatoes or two large
½ cup	minced red or green onions
½ cup	red bell peppers, chopped
1 Tbsp.	lime or lemon juice, freshly squeezed
1 clove	garlic, peeled and minced
¼ cup	fresh cilantro, minced
1 tsp.	apple cider vinegar
1 Tbsp.	raw unfiltered honey (optional)

Place all ingredients in a bowl and mix well. Let stand one hour to allow flavors to marry. Serve as a condiment or eat right out of the bowl!

Soups, Stews, and Chowders

"…The earth is full of the goodness of the Lord."
—Psalm 33:5

Trimming the tree was always such fun! Here I am at the age of four with my brother Terry, putting the finishing touches on our fragrant tree. As I recall, Mom was in the kitchen preparing goodies for the holidays.

VEGETABLE SOUP STOCK

★★★	Yield: 8 cups
3	carrots (2 if carrots are large)
1 bunch	green onions
2 or 3	zucchini
4 large cloves	garlic, peeled
2 large	organic onions, leave inner skin on if organic
3	celery ribs (stalks)
2 medium	potatoes with skin (if organic), scrubbed
1 cup	parsley
1 sprig	fresh thyme or ½ tsp. dried
1	bay leaf
1 sprig	fresh summer savory or ½ tsp. dried
8–10 cups	distilled water

Chop all vegetables, except garlic, in chunks. Place in stockpot with herb seasonings. Cover with cold water, bring to a boil, reduce heat, cover and simmer for 45 minutes. Remove from heat and allow to cool. Strain. Use for soups, stews, or as a base for sauces. May be frozen until needed. (I freeze mine in one-cup or two-cup containers so I can easily have access to the amount I need.)

Option: May add any vegetables that you have on hand except those that would add a strong flavor and overpower the others.

CREAMY CELERY SOUP

★★★★★	Serves 4–6
2 cups	almond milk (or other non-dairy milk)
1 cup	pine nuts*, soaked one hour and drained
1 bunch	celery
½	sweet onion, sliced thin
2 medium	tomatoes (one to puree, the other diced)
2 cups	vegetable soup stock
1 tsp.	paprika
	Herb seasonings to taste

Make almond milk by placing 1 cup of almonds in a Vita-Mix or blender and process until creamy. (If not using a Vita-Mix, the "milk" may need to be strained to remove pulp). Add drained pine nuts, half of the celery, the soup stock along with one tomato and process until pureed. Pour into a bowl. Dice the other tomatoes and chop the remaining celery to add to the soup stock along with the sliced onions and seasonings.

*Rhonda's Kitchen Tips: Pine nuts (pignoli or pignola) are the edible, soft, white seed of a number of western North American pine trees. They add versatility in the kitchen with a creamy consistency when used in sauces or dressings and a wonderful texture when used whole. Because pine nuts have a very short shelf life, they should be stored in the freezer.

WILD RICE AND VEGETABLE SOUP

★★★	Serves 14–16
4 quarts	vegetable soup stock (see recipe on page 60.)
2–3 cloves	garlic, peeled
¼ cup	dehydrated or sun dried (not oil packed) tomatoes, snipped into small pieces
2 large	carrots, halved and sliced thin
1 medium	parsnip or turnip, diced
1 cup	celery, thinly sliced
1 cup	green beans, trimmed and chopped
2	leeks, white part only, cleaned and thinly sliced
2 cups	cabbage, shredded
1 cup	wild rice, pre-cooked
1 cup	brown lentils, washed and picked over
4	new red potatoes, quartered
1 cup	fresh or frozen green peas
	Herb seasonings to taste
	Celtic Sea Salt® to taste (optional)
	Grated non-dairy Parmesan Cheese* (optional)

In a large stockpot, bring stock to boil. Reduce heat to simmer; add garlic and tomatoes. Stir, bringing back to steady simmer.

Add ingredients in the following order, bringing soup back to steady simmer between each addition: carrots, parsnip, celery, green beans, leeks, and cabbage. After adding cabbage, simmer 25 minutes.

Add rice, lentils, and potatoes all at once. Cover and simmer 35 minutes.

Add herb seasoning and Celtic Sea Salt®. Add green peas. Cook only until soup returns to a simmer. Serve with a dash of non-dairy Parmesan, if desired.

*Note: This soup can be made a couple of days ahead of time and stored in the refrigerator. Recipe becomes 1★ if using Parmesan Cheese.

ACORN SQUASH SOUP

★	Serves 8–10
4 cups	distilled water
2 medium	acorn squash, scrubbed, halved and seeds removed
1 large	onion, sliced
1 large	yellow bell pepper, seeded and chopped
3	apples peeled, cored and diced
1 tsp.	curry powder
1 tbsp.	Vegetarian Worcestershire sauce (optional)
3 cups	Vegetable Soup Stock (see recipe on page 60.)
2 cups	prepared non-dairy milk
	Celtic Sea Salt® (optional)
	Herb seasonings

In a large saucepan, bring water to a boil. Add squash, cover and boil 15 to 20 minutes until tender. Remove squash from pan, saving the liquid, and allow squash to cool. When the squash is cool enough to handle, scoop out the flesh and discard the skin.

In a large saucepan, lightly steam onion and bell pepper until onion is transparent. Add squash, reserved liquid, apples, curry, Worcestershire sauce, and vegetable broth. Add herb seasonings of choice. Bring to a boil; reduce heat to a simmer. Partially cover and cook for 15 minutes stirring occasionally.

Allow mixture to cool thoroughly.

Place squash mixture in a blender or food processor and puree. Return to saucepan. Stir in non-dairy milk, adjust seasonings and cook over medium heat just until heated through. DO NOT ALLOW TO BOIL.

CORN CHOWDER

★	Serves 5–6
1 medium	onion, chopped
2 large	baking potatoes, peeled and cubed
3 cups	distilled water, divided
1 cup	crackers, crushed into crumbs (Hain's crackers can be used)
3 cups	non-dairy milk
2 cups	frozen corn kernels
1 tsp.	Celtic Sea Salt® (optional)
1 tsp.	ground nutmeg

In a large saucepan steam sauté onions until translucent. Stir in potatoes and 2 cups of distilled water. Cook over medium heat until potatoes are tender. Combine cracker crumbs and milk substitute and stir into potato mixture. Stir in corn, salt, nutmeg, and remaining one cup of water. Reduce heat to medium-low and cook, stirring occasionally for approximately ten minutes or until heated through.

Option: Can run some of the corn through a food processor using an "S" blade before adding to the soup to make it creamier.

HARVEST TIME SOUP

★★★★★	Serves 4–6
4 cups	distilled water (or vegetable soup stock), heated but not boiling
4 cups	carrots, chopped
2–4 stalks	broccoli, peeled and chopped (or 2 cups florets)
2 large	yams or sweet potatoes, chopped
1 large	sweet onion, chopped
8	celery ribs (stalks), chopped
	Herb seasoning to taste

In Vita-Mix or blender, combine water or vegetable soup stock and carrot; blend well. Add broccoli; blend well. Add yam; blend well. Add onion, celery, and herb seasoning to taste.

RAW FRUIT SOUP
Peter Lynch (age 12)

★	Serves 1
1	ripe banana, peeled
1	apple, peeled and cored
	Any other fruit of choice (I like peaches)
4 tbsp.	raw almond butter
1 tbsp.	raw unfiltered honey*
½ tsp.	pure vanilla
½ tsp.	fresh lemon juice
½ tsp.	cinnamon

Blend all ingredients in a blender, Vita-Mix, Cuisinart, or other food processor using the "S" blade.

*Option: Replace 1 tbsp. honey with 2 soaked, pitted, and pureed dates and this becomes a 4-star (★★★★) recipe.

RAW SWEET POTATO SOUP

★★★★★	Serves 4–6
1 cup	vegetable soup stock (See recipe on page 60.) or distilled water
3 cups	sweet potato, grated
1 cup	celery, finely chopped
¼ cup	onion, diced
¼ cup	fresh parsley, minced (or 1 tsp. dried)
1 cup	fresh carrot juice
½ tsp.	dill weed
½ tsp.	all-purpose herb blend
	Celtic Sea Salt® to taste (optional)

Grate sweet potatoes, chop celery and onion, and mince parsley. Place half of the sweet potato, celery, and parsley, along with all of the onion and soup stock in a blender or food processor and blend until smooth. Stir in carrot juice and seasonings. Add the remaining vegetables, stir and serve. Garnish each bowl with minced parsley.

RAW VEGETABLE SOUP

★★★★★	Serves 4
4 cups	distilled water, heated but not to boiling
1 medium	carrot, cut in ½-inch pieces
1	celery rib (stalk) (with leaves), cut in 1-inch pieces
2	chopped green scallions or some chopped sweet onion
2 cups	fresh or frozen cherry tomatoes
	Herb seasoning to taste
	Celtic Sea Salt® or sea vegetables (dulse, kelp, etc.) to taste

Place all ingredients in Vita-Mix or other blender and blend until creamy.

Option: Chop some of the vegetables into bite size pieces and place them in the serving bowls. Blend the remaining ingredients and fill the bowl with the blended liquid for a crunchy delightful warm soup. Serve with dehydrated Raw Italian Bread Sticks (see recipe on page 172).

Option: During warm weather, use cold water and chill soup for a refreshing cold soup.

QUICK VEGETABLE SOUP
Nelly Bonfigli

★★★	Serves 4–6
2 cups	distilled water
1 large	onion, peeled
1 cup	white beans, cooked and drained
2	tomatoes
1	red bell pepper, seeded
2	carrots
2 cloves	garlic, peeled and minced

Chop all vegetables very small. Bring water to boil; add veggies and beans. Boil for 20 minutes, adding more water if necessary.

GAZPACHO SOUP

★★★★★	Serves 2–3
1	cucumber, peeled
2 large	ripe tomatoes, quartered
2 cups	fresh vegetable juice
1 tsp.	Celtic Sea Salt® (optional)
	Juice of ½ lemon
1–2 tbsp.	extra virgin cold pressed olive oil or Udo's oil or flaxseed oil
	Herb seasoning to taste

Combine in a food processor, Vita-Mix, or blender and blend until liquefied. Pour into a large bowl and add any or all of the following chopped or shredded vegetables, or those of your choosing.

1 clove	garlic, peeled and minced
1½ cups	fresh scallions or green onion
1	red, orange, or yellow bell pepper, seeded
2	celery ribs (stalks)
1 large	carrot
1 medium	yellow or zucchini squash
1 large	or 2 small ripe avocados, peeled and pitted

Garnish with chopped fresh parsley or cilantro and serve immediately.

CURRIED BUTTERNUT SQUASH SOUP
Jackie Graff, R.N., B.S.N

★	Serves 8
1 cup	Medjool dates, pitted and soaked in 1 cup distilled water for 2–3 hours and drained
1 tsp.	cinnamon
1 tsp.	cumin
1 inch	fresh gingerroot
1 tsp.	Celtic Sea Salt®
3 cloves	garlic, peeled
1 tsp.	cayenne pepper
2 tsp.	curry
1 tsp.	mustard powder
1 tbsp.	orange zest*
2 cups	fresh orange juice
1 cup	distilled water
1	avocado, peeled and pitted
1	onion
4 cups	butternut squash, peeled and cubed
½ cup	pumpkin seeds, washed, soaked for 8 hours, drained and dehydrated for 6–8 hours

Place all ingredients in Vita-Mix or blender and process until creamy.

***Rhonda's Kitchen Tips:** Zest is the colored part of the citrus fruit (oranges, lemons, limes, grapefruit, etc.). Use the fine side of a grater or a zesting tool that can be found in kitchen stores.

BLUSHING TOMATO SOUP

★★★★★	Serves 2
1 large	vine ripened tomato
1 medium	cucumber, peeled and seeded
½	sweet red bell pepper, seeded
1 tsp.	herb seasoning
1 tsp.	dried dill weed
½ tsp.	Celtic Sea Salt® or kelp (optional)
1 tsp.	chives, minced
1 tsp.	parsley, minced

Place tomato in Vita-Mix or blender and blend at low speed until creamy. Add cucumber and red pepper and blend until desired consistency is reached. Add seasonings and mix well. Cover and chill. Just before serving, garnish with chopped chives and/or parsley.

CUCUMBER DILL SOUP
Deborah Martin

★★★★★	Serves 4–6
1 large	cucumber, peeled, seeded, and cut into chunks
1 small clove	garlic, peeled
¼ cup	fresh dill
2 tbsp.	sweet onion, chopped
3 tbsp.	fresh lemon juice
½ tsp.	Celtic Sea Salt® (optional)

In a blender, combine all of the above ingredients and blend until smooth. Chill before serving.

Options: Add an avocado if you would like a soup that is heavier or use as a wonderful summer salad dressing.

VEGETABLE STEW

★★	Serves 4–6
Vegetables:	
3 cloves	garlic, minced
1 large	onion, chopped
2	celery ribs (stalks) cut on the diagonal
4 medium	carrots cut into rounds or small chunks
1 small	red or orange sweet bell pepper, seeded and chopped

Steam the above vegetables until al denté (firm but tender), then stir in the following vegetables and flour. Stir well to make sure all vegetables get a flour coating. When all of the vegetables are well coated, gently pour in vegetable broth and herbs. Do not stir. Cover and cook over lowest heat while you prepare the gravy ingredients.

3 cups	potatoes, peeled, and cut into chunks
2 cups	sweet apple, peeled and diced
4 small	butternut squash, peeled, seeded, and cubed
2 tbsp.	whole-grain flour
1	bay leaf
1 cup	vegetable soup stock
¼ tsp.	dried rosemary
½ tsp.	dried marjoram
1 tsp.	dried thyme
Gravy:	
2	low sodium vegetable bouillon cubes
3–4	dates, pitted
1 tbsp.	lemon juice or raw unfiltered apple cider vinegar
3 cups	butternut squash, cubed
3 cups	distilled water
1 tsp.	Celtic Sea Salt® (optional)
2 tbsp.	molasses (not Blackstrap)

In a blender or Vita-Mix place all gravy ingredients and process until smooth. Pour over the vegetables; bring to a boil, adding additional herb seasonings, if needed. Reduce heat to low, cover, and simmer for 60 minutes, stirring occasionally. Serve with homemade bread or rolls.

HOMEMADE "CREAM" SOUP

★	Yield: Equivalent to 9 cans of soup

To use in place of canned cream soups in casseroles or as a base for your own soups.

2 cups	non-dairy milk powder
¾ cup	Arrowroot Powder
¼ cup (or less)	low sodium vegetable bouillon
2 tbsp.	dried onion flakes
1 tsp.	dried basil leaves
1 tsp.	dried thyme leaves
Pinch	cayenne pepper

Combine all ingredients, mixing well. Store in an airtight container until ready to use. To substitute for one can of condensed soup, combine ⅓ cup of dry mix with 1¼ cups of cold distilled water in saucepan. Cook and stir until thickened. Add to casserole as you would the canned product. Makes equivalent of 9 cans of soup.

Variations:

Asparagus Soup: Add 1 cup chopped asparagus, cooked
Celery Soup: Add ½ cup celery, minced
Potato Soup: Add 1 cup diced potatoes, cooked
Vegetable Soup: Add ¾ cup mixed vegetables, cooked
Broccoli Soup: Add 1 cup chopped broccoli, cooked
Mushroom Soup: Add ½ cup mushrooms, finely chopped

The variations are endless, limited only to your imagination.

POTATO-VEGETABLE CHOWDER

★★★	Serves 8

Make as thick or thin as desired by adjusting the liquid.

5 cups	vegetable soup stock (see recipe on page 60.) (May use distilled water but soup will not be as flavorful)
1 cup	tomato or vegetable juice
1 cup	tomatoes, peeled and cut in small pieces
1 cup	carrots, chopped
1 cup	green beans or yellow wax beans, cut on diagonal
1 cup	onions, finely chopped
1 cup	zucchini or yellow squash, thinly sliced
1 cup	leeks, chopped
½ cup	corn kernels (optional)
3 cups	red potatoes, peeled and diced
	Fresh herbs of choice (parsley, basil, oregano, etc.)
2 tsp.	Celtic Sea Salt® (optional)

Bring liquid to boil in a deep soup kettle. Add all vegetables and seasonings. Turn down heat to simmer and partially cover the pot. Simmer until vegetables are tender. Remove ⅓ of the soup, cool* and place in food processor with an "S" blade or blender and puree. Add back to the soup and mix well. Serve hot with crusty whole-wheat bread and a light fruit dessert.

Options: Almost any vegetable but onions, tomatoes, and the potatoes can be substituted for another vegetable. The cabbage family flavors will radically change the flavor and are not recommended. Green peas and baby lima beans are great additions.

*Note: It is important to allow the soup to cool before blending as the steam may build up and blow the lid off the blender and scald someone!

CREAM OF TOMATO SOUP

Jackie Graff, R.N., B.S.N, Raw Foods Chef

★★★★★	Serves 4–6
1 cup	pine nuts*, soaked in distilled water for one hour, discard water
1 tsp.	cayenne pepper (optional)
2 tsp.	Celtic Sea Salt® (optional)
1 cup	sun-dried tomatoes, soaked in 2 cups distilled water for one hour
5 cups	fresh tomatoes
	Distilled water for desired consistency

Place pine nuts, sun-dried tomatoes with soak water, sea salt, and cayenne pepper in Vita-Mix or blender and blend until creamy. Add fresh tomatoes to the blender and blend until soup is creamy. If soup is too thick, slowly add distilled water until desired consistency is reached. Soup may be placed in dehydrator at 105 degrees for 15–30 minutes to warm.

***Rhonda's Kitchen Tips:** Pine nuts (pignoli or pignolia) are the edible, soft, white seed of a number of western North American pine trees. They add versatility in the kitchen with a creamy consistency when used in sauces or dressings and a wonderful texture when used whole. Because pine nuts have a very short shelf life, they should be stored in the freezer.

RAW BROCCOLI SOUP

★★★★★	Serves 4
1 cup	pine nuts*
2 cups	broccoli florets
2 tbsp.	sweet onion, chopped
¼ cup	fresh cilantro
½	avocado, peeled and pitted
½ tsp.	Celtic Sea Salt® (optional)
1 tsp.	herb seasoning
3 cups	hot distilled water (not boiling)

Place all ingredients in a Vita-Mix or blender and process until creamy.

Rhonda's Kitchen Tips: Pine nuts (pignoli or pignolia) are the edible, soft, white seed of a number of western North American pine trees. They add versatility in the kitchen with a creamy consistency when used in sauces or dressings and a wonderful texture when used whole. Because pine nuts have a very short shelf life, they should be stored in the freezer.

AVOCADO SOUP

★★★★★	Serves 4
3 small	avocados, peeled and pitted
2 cups	fresh tomato juice
1 cup	fresh carrot juice
1 small	sweet onion, chopped fine
1 cup	raw corn kernels
1 tbsp.	extra virgin cold pressed olive oil
1 cup	cherry tomatoes, halved or quartered
1 tsp.	cumin
½ tsp.	chili powder
Pinch	cayenne pepper (optional)
	Celtic Sea Salt® to taste (optional)

Place avocados, 2 cups of tomatoes, and carrot juice in a blender or Vita-Mix and process until pureed. Remove from blender and place in a bowl and fold in remaining ingredients.

VEGAN SPLIT PEA SOUP

★★★	Serves 6–8
1 pound	organic split peas, soaked overnight and drained
2 quarts	vegetable soup stock (see recipe on page 60.)
2 large	potatoes, peeled and shredded
1	leek, sliced
3	celery ribs (stalks), chopped
2 large	organic carrots, shredded or sliced
1	yellow onion, chopped
	Celtic Sea Salt® to taste (optional)
1 tsp.	garlic powder or to taste
1 tsp.	ground cumin or to taste
Pinch	cayenne pepper (optional)
½ cup	dried parsley
	Distilled water, add to soup if too thick

Soak peas overnight and drain. Place all ingredients in a large stockpot and bring to a boil. Turn down heat and simmer for 45 minutes or until split peas are soft. Transfer about ⅓ of the mixture to a blender and cool*. before blending to a creamy consistency and adding back into the soup. If a creamy soup is desired, allow soup to cool, then transfer all soup to blender in batches and blend to desired consistency. Serve with a leafy green salad and warm whole-grain bread.

*Note: It is important to allow the soup to cool before blending as the steam may build up and blow the lid off the blender and scald someone!

PUMPKIN SOUP
Jan Jenson

★	Serves 4–6
2 cups	vegetable soup stock (see recipe on page 60.)
2	green onions, chopped
2 cups	pumpkin or butternut squash or yams, cooked and mashed
½ cup	celery, chopped
¾ cup	non-dairy milk
1	bay leaf
1 tbsp.	salt-free tomato paste
	Chopped fresh parsley
Dash	nutmeg

Steam sauté onion and celery in a small amount of distilled water. Stir in tomato paste, vegetable soup stock, pumpkin, bay leaf, and seasonings. Simmer 30 minutes. Add non-dairy milk just before serving; heat until warm, but DO NOT BOIL. Sprinkle with chopped fresh parsley and a dash of nutmeg for color and flavor.

Options: May add any of the following: Italian herbs, fresh crushed garlic or garlic powder, or herb seasoning.

Salads

*"Build ye houses, and dwell in them; and plant gardens,
and eat the fruit of them."*

—*Jeremiah 29:5*

---

*'Twas the night before Christmas and all through the house...'
I just love this picture of George at age 4, seated on his Dad's
lap engrossed in a story.*

How To Build A Salad

1. Select dark green leafy lettuce, kale, spinach, endive, bok choy, or other dark leafy greens (iceberg lettuce contains minimal nutrients and is therefore not recommended).

2. Wash, drain, and wrap greens in a clean towel (not a paper towel, since some are coated with formaldehyde) then place in refrigerator to crisp.

3. While greens are crisping, clean and prepare the rest of the vegetables, then set aside.

4. Remove chilled lettuce and other greens from towel and tear into bite size pieces (using a knife bruises the lettuce and greens).

5. Fill the serving bowls half full of greens and then add layers of your favorite prepared vegetables.

6. Some vegetables to be considered:

    - Kohlrabi, grated
    - Radishes, chopped or sliced
    - Asparagus, fresh
    - Tomatoes, Cherry or chopped
    - Sweet corn, raw
    - Snow peas, raw
    - Sweet potatoes or yams, grated
    - Turnips, grated
    - Jicama, grated
    - Beets, grated
    - Red or green cabbage, chopped
    - Garlic or regular chives, chopped
    - Parsley, minced
    - Broccoli florets, small
    - Red onion, finely chopped
    - Green onion or scallions, chopped
    - California carrots, grated
    - Avocado*, diced
    - Celery, finely diced
    - Cucumber, sliced or diced
    - Cauliflower, small florets
    - Bell peppers, diced red or yellow

- Turnips, grated
- Zucchini, grated or chopped fine
- Cabbage, red or green grated or chopped fine
- Chives, regular or garlic, chopped
- Yellow squash, grated or chopped fine

Note: It is better not to use seeds and nuts in the same salad with avocado. Using seeds, nuts, and avocados at the same time gives the body too much fat to digest at one meal. When not using avocado some seeds and nuts that might be used are sunflower seeds, chopped walnuts, almonds, or pecans.

CRANAPPLE SALAD

★	Serves 2
1 cup	organic cranberries
2 large	sweet apples, peeled and chopped
3	organic Medjool dates (or 8 small dates)
¼ cup	nuts (walnuts, pecans, or your favorite)
¼ cup	raw unfiltered honey*
1 tbsp.	organic orange zest**
Pinch	Celtic Sea Salt® (optional)
¼ tsp.	cinnamon or pumpkin pie spice
	Pinch of ginger and allspice (optional)

Place apples in a food processor with an "S" blade and process until coarse consistency is reached. Add remaining ingredients and pulse until desired consistency is reached. Place in a non-metal bowl, cover and refrigerate for flavors to mingle.

*Option: Increase the dates and omit the honey and this becomes a 4-star (★★★★) recipe.

Rhonda's Kitchen Tips: Zest is the colored part of the citrus fruit (oranges, lemons, limes, grapefruit, etc.). Use the fine side or a grater or a zesting tool that can be found in kitchen stores.

LUSCIOUS CRANBERRY SALAD

Juanita Thomas

★★★★	Serves 4
1 cup	ground organic cranberries
1 cup	ground organic apple with peel
1½ cups	ground organic orange with peel
½ cup	crushed pineapple (packed in it's own juice)
1	banana, peeled and mashed

If no grinder is available, a food processor with an "S" blade or a blender may be used. Mix ingredients and cover in non-metal bowl. Let set for a couple of days. There is too much tartness if used immediately, but it blends as it sets. Even my junk food relatives like this one!

CRANBERRY FRUIT SALAD

★	Serves 4
1 tsp.	orange zest from organic orange*
1	organic orange, peeled and sectioned
1	tart apple, peeled, cored, and diced
1 cup	organic cranberries
⅓ cup	date sugar or maple syrup or raw unfiltered honey
1 cup	seedless grapes, halved
¾ cup	fresh pineapple (or pineapple packed in it's own juice)

Combine all ingredients in a bowl. Cover and chill until ready to serve.

Rhonda's Kitchen Tips: Zest is the colored part of the citrus fruit (oranges, lemons, limes, grapefruit, etc.). Use the fine side of a grater of a zesting tool that can be found in kitchen stores.

FRUIT SALAD WITH PINE NUT CRÈME

★★★★★

Make a big bowl of Fruit Salad; you might include sliced bananas, chopped apples, seedless grapes, and fresh strawberries. Top with Pine Nut Crème (see recipe on page 54).

RAW APPLE, PEAR, PECAN SALAD

★★★★	Serves 2
The Salad:	
3	celery ribs (stalks)
2	Red Delicious apples
1	Golden Delicious apple
1	pear
1	lemon
1	orange
¼ cup	dates, chopped
½ cup	raw pecans, chopped

Chop celery fine and put into bowl. Peel and chop apples and pear into small pieces. Juice lemon and orange and pour over apples and pear to keep them from turning brown. Stir to coat all fruit, and marinade for 10 minutes. Drain, saving juice.

While the fruit is soaking, chop pecans and dates. Add half of the chopped pecans along with the dates and celery to the drained fruit.

The Dressing:

Make dressing by combining the other half of the pecans in a blender or food processor with the reserved juice and puree into a nut butter sauce. Add puree to the salad and stir to blend all flavors. Serve on a bed of leaf lettuce.

CARROT APPLE SLAW

Ann

★★★★★	Serves 2
10	baby carrots (or one large carrot)
1	Fuji apple (or other sweet apple)
1 tsp.	cinnamon (or to taste)

Peel and shred carrots; peel skin off apple and shred. Add cinnamon, toss, and eat.

RAW CABBAGE/APPLE/DATE/NUT SALAD
Martha Jensen

★	Serves 4
½ head	red or green cabbage, shredded
1 cup	celery, diced
1	sweet apple, diced
1 cup	organic raisins
18	dates, diced (Medjool dates work well)
1 cup	walnuts or pecans, broken into large pieces
	Juice of one lemon
	Raw unfiltered honey to taste*

Place all ingredients in a bowl, mix, chill, and serve.

*Option: Omit honey and this becomes a 4-star (★★★★) recipe.

BANANA-PEAR-PECAN AMBROSIA
Dawn Lucie

★
Ripe bananas, cut into thin slices
Ripe pears*, cut into small chunks
Raw pecans*, whole or chopped
Maple syrup to taste**

Prepare fruit and nuts for the number of people being served. Drizzle with maple syrup before serving. Can be made in individual serving dishes or in a large bowl.

*Option: Use apples and walnuts instead of pears and pecans. It's better than apple pie!

**Option: Replace maple syrup with 2–3 soaked, pitted, and puréed dates and this becomes a 5-star (★★★★★) recipe.

SPICY TOMATO SALAD
Alice Lane

★	Serves 6
3 large	firm ripe tomatoes, chopped
1	bell pepper, seeded and chopped
1	sweet red onion, chopped
1 tsp.	raw unfiltered honey*
2 tbsp.	raw unfiltered apple cider vinegar
½ tsp.	ground cinnamon
½ tsp.	ground ginger
½ tsp.	ground allspice
⅛ tsp.	ground cloves
Pinch	Celtic Sea Salt® (optional)

Place all ingredients in a bowl, mix well, cover and refrigerate to allow flavors to mingle.

*Option: Replace honey with 1–2 soaked, pitted, and pureed dates and this becomes a 5-star (★★★★★) recipe.

SPINACH AND GRAPEFRUIT SALAD
Pat Ellis

★★★★	Serves 2–3
Large	handful of baby spinach
1	avocado, peeled, pitted, and cut into bite size pieces
⅓ head	cauliflower, broken into florets
1	grapefruit, peeled and cut into chunks
2 tbsp.	extra virgin cold pressed olive oil

Make a bed of the spinach. Toss other ingredients to mix well and serve on spinach bed.

RED CABBAGE AND FRUIT SALAD

Mrs. U. Gardiner

★★★★	Serves 4
½	thinly shredded medium red cabbage (or ¼ red cabbage and ¼ green cabbage)
1 small	sweet onion thinly sliced and chopped
1	orange, pitted and diced
1	sweet apple, peeled and diced
1	sweet banana, thinly sliced
	Juice of ½ lemon to pour over banana slices
Small	handful of organic raisins

Shred cabbage and prepare other solid ingredients except bananas. Slice bananas and pour lemon juice over them. Allow lemon juice to absorb for a couple of minutes and then combine all solid ingredients. Good with Orange Dressing (see recipe on page 114). Pour dressing on salad just before serving and mix well.

FINGER FOOD SALAD

★★★★★	
	Celery sticks
	Carrot sticks
	Zucchini sticks
	Cherry tomatoes
	Raw broccoli florets
	Raw cauliflower florets
	Guacamole Dip (see recipe on page 44.)

Place cut vegetables around outside of platter. Set a dish of guacamole dip in the center and enjoy.

RAW SWEET POTATO SALAD
Lois I. Duke

★★★★

Peel and finely shred raw sweet potato. To each cup of shredded sweet potato, add:

3–4	dates, finely chopped
⅓ cup	apples, finely chopped
2 tbsp.	walnuts or pecans, coarsely chopped
1 tsp.	orange zest*
¼ cup	fresh orange juice
Sprinkle	mace**

Toss and serve.

Rhonda's Kitchen Tips: Zest is the colored part of the citrus fruit (oranges, lemons, limes, grapefruit, etc.). Use the fine side of a grater or a zesting tool that can be found in kitchen stores.

****Rhonda's Kitchen Tips:*** Mace and nutmeg are the only spices that come from the same tropical evergreen tree, which grows in the East and West Indies. Mace is made from the lacy covering of the seed and is orange in color. Nutmeg, on the other hand, is made from the seed. Both spices add a warm, subtle, spicy flavor and may be used interchangeably.

HOLIDAY SWEET POTATO SLAW

★★★★	*Serves 2–3*
3 cups	sweet potatoes, raw and shredded
1 medium	sweet apple, peeled and chopped
1 cup	fresh pineapple tidbits
½ cup	pecans or walnuts, chopped
¼ cup	organic raisins or dates, chopped (optional)

In a large bowl, combine sweet potatoes, apple, pineapple, nuts, raisins or dates and set aside. Prepare the Holiday Slaw Dressing (see recipe on page 113). Combine with salad and mix well.

PUMPKIN SALAD

Faye Pulvermuller

★★★★	Serves 4
12 ounces	pumpkin flesh, peeled and finely diced
2	apples, cored and diced
4	celery ribs (stalks), sliced thinly
¼ cup	walnuts, chopped (or nuts of choice)
½ cup	raisins, soaked in distilled water (could use dried cranberries, soaked)
Sprinkle	cinnamon, nutmeg, or cardamom (optional)

Combine ingredients in a bowl and set aside.

Combine with Sweet Lemon Dressing (see recipe on page 112) and mix well. Cover and chill salad in the refrigerator for about 30 minutes. Serve over a bed of greens.

WILD RICE SALAD

★★★★★	Serves 6
4 cups	wild rice, soaked 48 hours and drained
½	cucumber
1 cup	frozen or fresh peas
1 cup	ripe bell pepper (red, yellow, etc.), seeded
½ cup	shredded carrot
1 medium	tomato
1	celery rib (stalk)
½ cup	sweet red onion or scallions
1 - 2 tsp.	dried parsley or basil
1 - 2 tbsp.	kelp, to taste

Pour enough distilled water over wild rice to cover, place a towel or lid over bowl and soak 48 hours. Drain rice and rinse well then place in a large bowl. Shred carrots and chop remaining ingredients fine; mix in seasonings and add to rice.

Combine with Avocado Dressing (see recipe on page 114), stir well and serve immediately.

SQUASH AND GREENS

★★★★★	Serves 3 or 4
1 cup	zucchini, grated
1 cup	crookneck squash, grated
1 cup	carrots, grated
½ cup	red bell pepper, seeded and chopped
½ cup	chives or sweet onion, chopped

Toss all ingredients and serve on a bed of fresh greens with your favorite dressing.

HOMEMADE POTATO SALAD

★★★	Serves 6
The Salad:	
4 large	red potatoes
2	celery ribs (stalks)
½	red bell pepper, seeded
½	sweet red onion
The Dressing:	
2	ripe avocados, peeled and pitted
	Fresh or dried dill
	Lemon Juice

Steam the whole potatoes until just tender. Remove skins and allow them to cool. When cooled cut into one-inch cubes. Dice celery then bell pepper and onion and add to cubed potatoes.

Make dressing of avocados mashed with lemon juice and fresh dill or other herbs to taste. Gently mix all ingredients together.

MOSTLY RAW POTATO SALAD

★★★	Serves 6
4	potatoes
¼ cup	celery, diced
1 cup	carrot, grated
¼ cup	sweet red onion, diced
¼ cup	sweet red bell pepper, seeded and diced
2 tbsp.	raw flaxseed oil (or Udo's Oil Blend)
¼ cup	organic apple juice
1 tsp.	all purpose herb seasoning
	Celtic Sea Salt® to taste (optional)

Boil potatoes until almost soft. While boiling potatoes, prepare the other vegetables. When potatoes are done, run cold water into the potato pot until the potatoes are cool. Drain. Cube potatoes into a large mixing bowl; add raw vegetables, oil, apple juice, and seasonings. Mix and refrigerate for at least an hour before serving.

APPLE/NUT AND GREENS SALAD

★★★★	Serves 2
1 handful	baby salad greens
2	Golden Delicious apples, peeled and diced
¼ cup	pecans, cut into large pieces
1	celery rib (stalk), diced
	Juice of one orange
1 tbsp.	extra virgin cold pressed olive oil

Place greens in bottom of bowl. Add diced apple, then celery, and top with pecans. Place orange juice and olive oil in a blender, small jar with a lid, or use a small wire whisk and combine in a bowl. Pour dressing over salad.

Option: May add a few organic raisins for a sweeter flavor.

MANGO JICAMA SALAD
Patricia Lee

★★★★	Serves 6–8
2 heads	each red oak leaf and Boston lettuce, washed and torn up
1	red onion, halved and finely sliced
2	firm mangos, peeled and cut into ¾ inch cubes
1	jicama, peeled and cut in ¼ x 2-inch strips
2	avocados, peeled, pitted and sliced

Place the lettuce leaves, onion, mangos, and jicama in salad bowl; top with avocado slices. No dressing required.

Option: If you do not have jicama, you can substitute water chestnuts.

CABBAGE CRUNCH SALAD
Carolyn R. Faulk

★★	Serves 4
1 cup	sliced almonds, toasted
4 cups	green cabbage, shredded small
1 bunch	green spring onions, diced
½ package	chow mein noodles
4 tsp.	sesame seeds

Place the sliced almonds in a pan and bake in the oven at 375 degrees for 15 minutes to toast. Remove from oven and set aside to cool. While almonds are cooling, clean spring onions and chop. Remove outer leaves of cabbage and shred. Place onions and cabbage in a large bowl.

In a small bowl combine the cooled toasted almonds with the chow mein noodles and sesame seeds, and sprinkle over salad.

Just before serving, top with Carolyn's Honey Mustard Dressing (see recipe on page 116) and mix well.

FESTIVITY SALAD
Tamima Levin

★★★★★	Serves 4
1 large	carrot, grated
1 large	beet, grated
1 large	sweet apple, grated
1 cup	almonds, soaked overnight, drained, dehydrated and coarsely chopped*
	Juice of 1 lemon

Toss veggies and nuts together in large bowl. Drizzle on lemon juice and mix well. Serve on a bed of torn lettuce leaves.

Rhonda's Kitchen Tips: Almonds may be soaked, dehydrated, and frozen so they are ready to use when needed.

APPLE AND PINEAPPLE SALAD
Valerie Mills Daly

★	Serves 2
2 large	Granny Smith Apples, cut into bite-size pieces
½ average	pineapple, cut into small chunks
½ cup	golden raisins
½ cup	celery, diced
½ cup	almonds, walnuts, or raw pecans (soaked and dehydrated), chopped
⅓ cup	Vegenaise® (or Rhonda's No-Oil Salad Dressing*)
2 tbsp.	raw unfiltered honey
2 tbsp.	fresh lemon juice
½ tsp.	cinnamon

Prepare fuit and celery, set aside. Chop nuts, set aside. Combine remaining ingredients, mixing well, and then blend into the fruit mixture. Cover and refrigerate until well chilled and add chopped nuts before serving.

*Note: The recipe for Rhonda's No-Oil Salad Dressing can be found in Recipes for Life ... from God's Garden.

LAYERED SALAD
Ray and Sam Eddy

★★★★★

Take any hard veggie you can find and wash it. For example:

Broccoli
Cauliflower
Carrot
Celery
Bok choy
Cabbage
Or other veggies of your choice

Place each item separately in a food processor and chop to BB size pieces. Empty each veggie into a bowl. Keep layering until you use all veggies. You have a beautiful layered salad that can be served immediately.

Option & Time Saver: To use salad for a few days, layer into a container that has a double layer of paper towels in the bottom, or vacuum-seal one package for each meal. Each time you need a salad, simply scoop out about a cup at a time and garnish with avocados, tomatoes, etc. and make a dressing of your own choice to use on it. This is a great food source!

TAMARI CABBAGE
Bruce and Eleanor Oyen

★

1 head	cabbage
	Tamari wheat-free soy sauce
	Extra virgin cold pressed olive oil
	Scallions (optional)

With a sharp knife, shred cabbage, and thinly slice scallions. Combine all ingredients in proportions pleasing to you. Mix thoroughly and enjoy.

CITRUSY SALAD
Michael Frumer

★

The Salad:

Grapefruit, sectioned and cut in pieces

Red grapes, cut in half

Carrot, shredded

Pecans, coarsely chopped

Sunflower seeds

Pepitas (pumpkin seeds)

Escarole (Endive) greens, cut in pieces or packaged mixed organic greens

Ripe avocado, peeled, pitted, and cubed, with the juice of ½ lemon squeezed over it

Place all ingredients except avocado in a salad bowl and mix well. Drain avocado (reserving juice for dressing) and gently fold avocado into the salad mixture. Set aside.

The Dressing:

¼ cup	grapefruit juice
	Juice from ½ of an orange
	Lemon juice that has been drained from the avocado
Pinch	cayenne pepper
2 tbsp.	Balsamic vinegar or raw unfiltered apple cider vinegar

Combine dressing ingredients, pour over salad, and gently mix to combine. Serve with whole-grain bread for a complete dinner.

Option: Replacing Balsamic vinegar with apple cider vinegar makes this a 4-star (★★★★)recipe.

ORANGE SUN SALAD

★	Serves 6
6 cups	carrots, shredded
8 oz.	green olives, halved and pitted
1–2 cloves	garlic, minced
½ cup	basil, chopped
2 tbsp.	lime juice
¼ cup	Vegenaise® (use more or less for desired consistency)

Mix all ingredients well and refrigerate before (and after) serving for best flavor.

Makes a delicious sandwich spread.

SPINACH & STRAWBERRY SALAD
Susan Wunsch

★★★★	Serves 4–6
	Fresh organic baby spinach (2 bunches or 1 bag)
1 pint	organic strawberries, sliced
1 small	red onion, sliced thin and cut into quarters
¼ cup	pecan pieces

Place ingredients in a bowl and mix well. Serve with Susan's Dressing (see recipe on page 118). Pour dressing over the salad just before serving. Toss.

AVOCADO FRUIT SALAD

★★★★	Serves 1
1	ripe banana, peeled and sliced
½	avocado, peeled, pitted, and diced
3–4	dates, pitted and diced
¼ cup	organic raisins, soaked in distilled water until plump (about 15 minutes)

Place all ingredients in a bowl and mix gently. Serve as is or on a bed of fresh salad greens.

SIMPLE CARROT SALAD
Hilde Buehler

★★★★★

Grate organic carrots with equal amount of grated organic apples

Mix well with wooden or plastic fork or spoon.

Drizzle with lemon juice (for preserving freshness)

Top with raw sunflower seeds.

The amounts depend on size of salad desired. I prepare this salad when I am really short on time to prepare a regular meal.

LETTUCE FREE SALAD
Chris Walters

★★★★★

Wash and slice the following: cucumber, carrots, tomato, red peppers, and avocado.

Toss them together in a bowl and enjoy. It is a lettuce free salad. It does not need salad dressing because the cucumber and tomato are moist and the avocado helps lots too.

UNIQUE COLESLAW
Nancy Clark-Hughey

★

Raw cabbage

Raw beet, peeled

Raw sweet potato, peeled

Raw turnip, peeled

Vegenaise®

Using a food processor, shred cabbage, beet, sweet potato, and turnip. This gives the slaw a really great taste and added nutrition. Mix with Vegenaise® (or other high quality mayo with flaxseed oil and no preservatives).

"GRACE'S" MOCK CRAB SALAD
Nancy Velardi Potts

★★★★★	Serves 4–6

My mom made this for me over 20 years ago.

4	carrots, peeled
1	parsnip, peeled
1 small	onion, peeled
2	celery ribs (stalks), cut into chunks
2 tbsp.	fresh parsley

Put all of the ingredients in the processor and flip the switch. I use some homemade mayonnaise (Vegenaise® or Rhonda's No-Oil Salad Dressing*) to hold it all together. Only a small amount is needed, just enough to hold everything together.

Serve it on whole-grain dinner rolls or on sweet bread. My mom liked it on potato rolls. Can also be served on a bed of baby greens with a zesty dressing.

This recipe can be increased using the same proportions.

*Note: The recipe for Rhonda's No-Oil Salad Dressing can be found in *Recipes for Life ... from God's Garden.*

SWEET POTATO SALAD
Belinda Yingst

★★★★★	Serves 1–2
1	sweet potato or yam, grated
⅓ cup	organic currants or raisins
½ cup	raw nuts, chopped or crushed

A splash of fresh apple juice to moisten it

Mix it all together and enjoy!

RAW STUFFED SQUASH
Francis Fischer

★★★★★	
	Zucchini or yellow squash
	Tomatoes
¼ tsp.	Celtic Sea Salt®
	Garlic Powder
	Basil
	Oregano
	Onion powder

Take as many raw zucchini or yellow squash as you like and scoop out the insides, right to the edge of the skin.

Put the insides of the zucchini or yellow squash in the Vita-Mix, blender, or food processor using the "S" blade along with a few tomatoes. Add about ¼ tsp. Celtic Sea Salt®, garlic powder, basil, oregano, and onion powder to taste. Whiz it up and pour it into the squash shells. Simple and great!

SPINACH SALAD WITH BERRIES
Ginny Glenn

★★★★	Serves 6
6 cups	fresh spinach (6 ounces) torn into bite size pieces
1 cup	strawberries, thickly sliced
1 cup	blueberries
1 small	red onion, thinly sliced
½ cup	pecans, chopped
	Herb seasoning to taste

Wash and dry spinach and place it in a bowl. Add berries, onion, and pecans, and herb seasoning if desired.

Top with Curry Dressing (see recipe on page 116). Toss lightly and serve.

MARINATED VEGGIE SALAD
Nancy Clark-Hughey

★★★★★

Use any combo of veggies you like and cut into bite size pieces any amount of the following:

Carrots
Celery
Green, red, yellow peppers
Cherry tomatoes
Black olives
Broccoli
Cauliflower
Pea pods
Asparagus
Water chestnuts
Red onions
Anything else you like

Marinate in Lemon Vinaigrette dressing (see recipe on page 119) or your own favorite vinaigrette dressing.

Keeps for 3–5 days in refrigerator.

EASY SPINACH SALAD
Nancy Clark-Hughey

★★★★

Spinach leaves, torn
Red onion, chopped
Almonds, slivered
Breadcrumbs, toasted

Place all ingredients in a bowl and top with a Raspberry Vinaigrette dressing (see recipe on page 119).

Option: You can make a dressing of lemon and extra virgin cold pressed olive oil.

"EAT THE COLOR SALAD"
Thomas Villalon

★★★★★

Make the salad out of:

Cauliflower (white)
Celery (green)
Carrots (orange)
Sweet bell pepper (red or yellow)
Cucumbers (light green)

Arrange the above fruits and vegetables on a plate, grouped by color. The object is to make the food on the plate pleasing to the eye. If you make a game out of it, the kids will tend to "play along" and eat it. At our house, this salad has eating rules. If there are 5 colors in the salad, I tell my kids they have to eat 4 out of 5, or 6 out of 7, etc.

MY SISTER-IN-LAW'S SALAD
Barbara M. Singer

★★★★★

Chop and combine the following in a bowl according to the number of people you plan to serve:

Cauliflower florets
Broccoli florets
Red onions, sliced thin
Raisins
Sunflower seeds

Mix the above with your favorite dressing and serve.

SQUASH SALAD
Barbara A. Waters

★★★★★	Serves 4–6
3 medium	summer squash
½	cucumber
1 medium	Vidalia onion
1 large	tomato
¼	bell pepper, seeded
1 tsp.	Italian seasoning
	Juice of ½ lemon
1 tsp.	Udo's oil and 1 tsp. extra virgin cold pressed olive oil
	Celtic Sea Salt® (optional)

Grate squash and chop other vegetables. Add remaining ingredients and enjoy!

RAW ORIENTAL SALAD
Judi Setzer

★★★★★	Serves 4–6

Here is one of my favorite raw vegetable recipes I have adapted from the Oriental Ramen Salad. It's just as good as the original recipe.

In a bowl combine and mix well the following:

5–8	carrots, shredded
1 head	cabbage, shredded
⅛ cup	green onions, chopped
1 tbsp.	raw sesame seeds
2 tbsp.	almonds, slivered

Mix together Judi's Ginger Dressing (see recipe on page 114) and pour over salad. Toss to mix well.

AVOCADO BOATS WITH HOMEMADE SALSA

Georgia Buckner

★★★★★	Serves 2
The Boat:	
1	ripe avocado
1	lettuce leaf

See Helpful Kitchen Tips, page 263, item #15 for tips on cutting an avocado. Cut avocado in half, remove and discard the seed. Remove the flesh and place the empty shell on the lettuce leaf and set aside.

The Stuffing:	
	Flesh of the avocado, diced
2 tbsp.	onion, chopped fine
2	Tomatillos or cherry tomatoes, chopped fine
½	tomato, chopped fine or pureed
¼	raw red bell pepper, seeded and finely chopped
¼ tsp.	fresh lime juice
1 clove	garlic, peeled and put through Garlic Press

Combine stuffing ingredients and mix well. Stuff avocado halves; they may need to be piled high!

SUMMER SALAD

Priscilla Warren

★★★★★	Serves 4–6
4 large	garden fresh tomatoes, chopped
2	cucumbers, chopped
1	red onion, chopped
1 tbsp.	raw unfiltered apple cider vinegar
	Celtic Sea Salt® (optional)
Pinch	cayenne pepper (optional)

Mix and enjoy, no dressing needed.

GREEK SALAD
Laura Curtiss

★★

Place the following ingredients in a bowl:

4 medium	tomatoes, cut into wedges
1	cucumber, peeled and sliced
½ small	red onion, sliced thin
Handful	of pitted Calamata olives (rinsed well)
¼ cup	extra virgin cold pressed olive oil
	Juice of 3 lemons
¼ tsp. each:	dried oregano, basil, Celtic Sea Salt® (can use fresh herbs)
	Fresh squeezed garlic to taste
Pinch	cayenne pepper, if desired

Let marinate for at least 30 minutes before serving for flavors to marry; stir before serving. Delicious!

RAW MEXICAN CORN SALAD
Deborah Martin

★★★★★	Serves 4–6
4 ears	raw sweet corn, cut off cob
1 cup	fresh Cilantro, chopped
1 cup	fresh Parsley, chopped
1 small	red onion, finely chopped
2	red bell peppers, seeded and chopped
2	yellow bell peppers, seeded and chopped
2	orange bell peppers, seeded and chopped
3	Roma tomatoes, cubed

Prepare all ingredients and place in bowl, mix well, and top with Raw Mexican Corn Salad Dressing (see recipe on page 116).

CUCUMBER AND AVOCADO SALAD

★★★★★	Serves 4–6
2	ripe avocados, peeled, pitted, and cut into chunks
1	vine ripened tomato, cut into chunks
2 medium	cucumbers, peeled, seeded and cut into chunks
½ cup	green onions, chopped
¼ cup	fresh dill, chopped
½ tsp.	Celtic Sea Salt® (optional)
¼ cup	fresh lime juice

Mix all together. The lime juice along with the avocado will create a wonderful dressing.

RED CABBAGE SALAD
Anita Jones

★	Serves 4–6
2 cups	red cabbage shredded
½ cup	pine nuts*, soaked ½ hour and drained
2	Minneola tangerines, peeled (or other tangerine)
2	green onions, chopped fine
3 tbsp.	extra virgin cold pressed olive oil
2 tbsp.	Balsamic vinegar (or fresh squeezed lemon juice)
2 tbsp.	fresh squeezed orange juice
	Celtic Sea Salt® to taste (optional)
	Nuts as garnish if desired

Carefully slice the tangerine crosswise and separate sections to arrive at tiny little juicy chunks. Toss together all ingredients and serve immediately or allow flavors to mingle by refrigerating for 30 minutes or more.

Rhonda's Kitchen Tips: Pine nuts (pignoli or pignolia) are the edible, soft, white seed of a number of western North American pine trees. They add versatility in the kitchen with a creamy consistency when used in sauces or dressings and a wonderful texture when used whole. Because pine nuts have a very short shelf life, they should be stored in the freezer.

RAW WALDORF SALAD
Linda Wetzel

★	Serves 6–8

Toss together the following ingredients (organic if possible):

8–10	celery ribs (stalks), washed and chopped into medium chunks (up to 1")
3–4 large	Red Delicious apples, unpeeled, cored, and cut into medium chunks as above
½ cup	raw sunflower seeds
1 cup	Vegenaise® (the grape seed oil variety)

Line a large serving bowl (clear glass is pretty with this) with washed and dried Romaine lettuce leaves or any similar type of lettuce or other greens.

Fill the lettuce-lined bowl with the "Waldorf" salad and it's done. Keep it cold, and enjoy!

MY RAW CABBAGE SALAD
Martha Jensen

★★★★★	Serves 4
½ medium	head green cabbage
1 cup	celery, diced
1	sweet apple, diced (Fireside apple is an excellent choice)
1 cup	organic raisins
18	Medjool dates, chopped
1 cup	broken walnuts and/or pecans
	Juice of one lemon
	Small amount of raw unfiltered honey (optional)

Each of the ingredients in this recipe can be altered, more or less, without changing the quality of it. It is good regardless and has been loved by everyone that has ever tried it.

FRUIT SALAD

★★★★	Serves 2–3
1	pear, peeled and chopped
1	apple, peeled and chopped
1 cup	fresh pineapple, chopped (optional)
1 cup	seedless grapes, cut in halves
1	banana, chopped
1	celery rib (stalk), chopped
¼ cup	organic dates, chopped
¼ cup	organic raisins
¼ cup	pecans, chopped
¼ cup	raw almonds, chopped

Prepare all ingredients and put in bowl. Mix well—no dressing required.

OUR MEXICALI SALAD

★★★★★	Serves 4–6
2 cups	fresh corn kernels
½ cup	fresh parsley, minced
½ cup	fresh Cilantro, minced
1 cup	scallions, chopped
1	cucumber, diced
1	red bell pepper, seeded and chopped
1	orange and/or yellow bell pepper, seeded and chopped
2	celery ribs (stalks), diced
1	Roma or a handful of cherry tomatoes, chopped

Prepare all ingredients and place in a bowl. Top with Mexicali Dressing (see recipe on page 117)..

SPICY RAINBOW SLAW

★★★★	Serves 6

Don't be intimidated by the number of ingredients in this spicy slaw.

3 cups	green cabbage, thinly sliced
1	red bell pepper, seeded and chopped
1	green pepper, seeded and chopped
1 small	red onion, thinly sliced
2 large	carrots, thinly julienned
1 cup	raw unfiltered apple cider vinegar
⅓ cup	fresh or organic apple juice
1 tsp.	celery seed
½ tsp.	turmeric
¼ tsp.	allspice
¼ tsp.	cinnamon
¼ tsp.	ginger
¼ tsp.	cloves
1 tbsp.	Celtic Sea Salt® (makes the vegetables weep and release their juices)
	pinch of cayenne pepper

In colander, mix cabbage, bell peppers, red onion, and carrots and sprinkle with salt. The salt helps to wilt the vegetables. Set aside for one hour. Rinse vegetables and drain well. Mix vinegar, apple juice, and spices and toss with vegetables. Cover and chill before serving.

POPEYE'S SPINACH SALAD

★★★★★	Serves 4–6
1 package	baby spinach leaves
1 medium	red, orange, or yellow bell pepper, seeded and diced
1	ripe tomato, diced
½	red onion, diced
1 cup	chopped nuts (walnuts, pecans, or your favorite)

Assemble and toss with Honey Mustard Dressing (see recipe on page 114) or your favorite.

Option: May substitute 1 cup red kidney or other beans, instead of chopped nuts

BROWN RICE SALAD
Valerie Sommers, Australia

★★★	Serves 4
2½ cups	brown long grain rice
1 cup	button mushrooms, sliced (optional)
1 clove	garlic, crushed
1	red bell pepper, seeded and chopped
2	celery ribs (stalks), sliced
2	spring onions, finely sliced
1 medium	avocado, peeled, pitted, and diced

Cook rice, drain well, rinse under cold water and drain well again. Set aside. Steam sauté, garlic, and mushrooms (if using) in a large pan. Cook, stirring, until vegetables are just tender; remove from heat and allow to cool.

Combine sautéed mixture with rice, bell pepper, celery, and spring onions in a large serving bowl; mix well. Just before serving, add avocado and drizzle with Valerie's Dressing (see recipe on page 117).

Dressings

"For the Lord thy God bringeth thee into a good land, a land of brooks of water, of fountains and depths that spring out of valleys and hills; A land of wheat, and barley, and vines, and fig trees, and pomegranates; a land of oil olive, and honey."

—Deuteronomy 8:7–8

A hint of things to come! Here I am with my first culinary creation! Mom and Dad had left us kids at home, and I decided to "entertain." Of course, when you have company, you bake a cake. I had seen my Mom whip up delightful desserts dozens of times, so how hard could it be? I threw together (and I do mean threw) everything I thought should go into a yummy cake. Eggshells, milk and flour were everywhere! When Mom came home and saw the "tornado" of ingredients that hit her kitchen, she gasped, "What happened here? I guess it's time I teach you to cook." Little did she know what she started. And, yes, I'm still a mess in the kitchen! But now, I clean up after myself!

For additional salad dressing recipes, see Rhonda's other books *Recipes for Life…from God's Garden* and *Salad Dressings for Life…from God's Garden*. *Salad Dressings for Life… from God's Garden* contains 117 different salad dressing recipes.

SWEET LEMON DRESSING
Faye Pulvermuller

★	Yield: Approximately ½ cup
½ cup	Vegenaise®
1 tbsp.	lemon juice
1 or 2 tbsp.	juice from soaked raisins

Place in small bowl and whisk to mix well. Stir into salad and mix well.

CREAMY HERB & GARLIC DRESSING
Tanya Fleming

★★★★★	Yield: Approximately 1 cup
1 clove	garlic, peeled and chopped fine
sprinkle	dehydrated onion flakes
2 tsp.	fresh oregano, minced
¼ cup	extra virgin cold pressed olive oil
	Juice of ½ lemon
1 rounded tsp.	tahini
¼ tsp.	Celtic Sea Salt® or to taste (optional)

Shake all ingredients together and serve over your choice of salad.

EASY AVOCADO DRESSING
Brenda-Joyce Garner

★★★★★	Yield: Approximately ½ cup
½ large	avocado, peeled and pitted
1 ounce	lime juice
1 tsp.	kelp

Blend or mash avocado until a creamy consistency is reached. Stir in lime juice and kelp.

Good with fruit or vegetable salad.

HOLIDAY SLAW DRESSING

★	Yield: Approximately ¾ cup
½ cup	Vegenaise®
1–2 tbsp.	raw unfiltered honey
2 tbsp.	fresh lemon juice
1 tsp.	lemon zest*

Combine ingredients into shaker cup and shake thoroughly or place in a bowl and whip with a wire whisk until well blended.

Rhonda's Kitchen Tips: Zest is the colored part of the citrus fruit (oranges, lemons, limes, grapefruit, etc.). Use the fine side of a grater or a zesting tool that can be found in kitchen stores.

OLE' DRESSING
Brenda-Joyce Garner

★★★★★	Yield: Approximately ½ cup
3 ounces	extra virgin cold pressed olive oil
1 clove	garlic, peeled and minced
1 ounce	lime juice
1 tbsp.	kelp

Combine ingredients into shaker cup and shake thoroughly or place in a bowl and whip with a wire whisk until well blended.

SHAY'S FRENCH DRESSING
Shay Hopper

★	Yield: Approximately 1¼ cups
1 cup	Vegenaise®
2 tbsp.	unsweetened catsup
1 tbsp.	raw unfiltered honey
1 tbsp.	dried basil
	Distilled water to thin, if needed

Combine all ingredients in a bowl and mix well. Store in a covered container in the refrigerator.

ORANGE DRESSING
Mrs. U. Gardiner

★	Yield: Approximately ½ cup
	Juice of one orange
1 tbsp.	raw unfiltered honey
2 tbsp.	flaxseed oil

Place ingredients in a small bowl and use a wire whisk to combine.

AVOCADO DRESSING

★★★★★	Yield: Approximately 2 cups
1	large avocado, peeled and pitted
½–1 cup	tomato juice
1–3 cloves	garlic, peeled and minced
	Pinch of cayenne, kelp or herbs to taste.

Mash avocado and fold in other ingredients. Serve immediately.

JUDI'S GINGER DRESSING
Judi Setzer

★	Yield: Approximately ¼ cup
¼ cup	rice vinegar
1 tsp.	Celtic Sea Salt® (optional)
1 tbsp.	grated fresh ginger

Combine ingredients and place in a small bowl or shaker jar and mix well. Pour over salad and enjoy.

HONEY MUSTARD DRESSING

★	Yield: Approximately ½ cup
2 tbsp.	Udo's Oil or extra virgin cold pressed olive oil
	Juice of one lemon
2 tsp.	stone ground salt-free mustard, or to taste
1 tsp.	raw unfiltered honey

Mix all ingredients with whisk or in food processor.

CAESAR DRESSING
Amanda Fallin

★	
½ cup	extra virgin cold pressed olive oil
½ cup	distilled water
2 ounces	raw unfiltered apple cider vinegar
4–5 shakes	balsamic vinegar
1 tsp.	Celtic Sea Salt® (optional)
1 packet	stevia or 1 tsp. other sweetener
1 tsp.	garlic powder
1 tsp.	onion powder
2 cloves	garlic, peeled and finely chopped
2 tbsp.	fresh parsley, finely chopped or 1 tsp. dried

Place all ingredients in a small bowl or shaker jar and mix well.

Options: May also be used on baked potatoes or lightly steamed vegetables.

SHAY'S RANCH DRESSING
Shay Hopper

★	Yield: Approximately 1 cup
1 cup	Vegenaise®
1 tbsp.	raw unfiltered apple cider vinegar
1 tsp.	raw unfiltered honey
1½ tsp.	dried chives
2 tsp.	Oriental Seasoning
¼ tsp.	onion powder

Combine all ingredients in a bowl and mix well. Store in a covered container in the refrigerator.

RAW MEXICAN CORN SALAD DRESSING
Deborah Martin

★★★★	Yield: Approximately ½ cup
¼ cup	lime juice
¼ cup	grape seed oil
1 tbsp.	fresh cilantro
¼ tsp.	chili powder
1 tsp.	Celtic Sea Salt® (optional)

Combine all ingredients in a small bowl use a wire whisk to mix well.

CURRY DRESSING
Ginny Glenn

★	Yield: Approximately ¼ cup
2 tbsp.	balsamic vinegar
2 tbsp.	rice vinegar
1 tbsp. plus 1 tsp.	raw unfiltered honey
1 tsp.	curry powder
2 tsp.	Dijon mustard

Combine all ingredients in a shaker jar or small bowl and mix well.

CAROLYN'S HONEY MUSTARD DRESSING
Carolyn R. Faulk

★	Yield: Approximately ¾ cup
½ cup	extra virgin cold pressed olive oil
6 tbsp.	raw unfiltered apple cider vinegar
4 tbsp.	raw unfiltered honey
½ tsp.	dry mustard
½ tsp.	Celtic Sea Salt® (optional)

Combine all ingredients in a shaker jar or small bowl and mix well.

MEXICALI DRESSING

★★★★	Yield: Approximately 1½ cup
½ cup	lemon juice
2	dehydrated apricots or 1 tbsp. fruit sweetened jam
½ cup	extra virgin cold pressed olive oil or grape seed oil
2 cloves	garlic, peeled
½ tsp.	cumin
½ tsp.	Italian Seasoning
	Celtic Sea Salt® to taste

Place first 4 ingredients in a blender or Vita-Mix and process until creamy. Pour into bowl and add remaining ingredients and whisk to blend.

SHAY'S HONEY MUSTARD DRESSING
Shay Hopper

★	Yield: Approximately 1½ cup
1 cup	Vegenaise®
2–3 tbsp.	stone-ground mustard
2–3 tbsp.	raw unfiltered honey
	Pinch of cayenne pepper (add slowly according to taste)

Combine all ingredients in a bowl and mix well. Store in a covered container in the refrigerator. If a thinner dressing is desired, slowly add distilled water to reach desired consistency.

VALERIE'S DRESSING
Valerie Sommers

★	Yield: Approximately ½ cup
¼ cup	lemon juice
¼ cup	extra virgin cold pressed olive oil
1 tsp.	raw unfiltered honey
2 tbsp.	stone-ground mustard
	Celtic Sea Salt® (optional)

Combine all ingredients in a screw-top jar; shake well.

SUSAN'S DRESSING
Susan Wunsch

★	Yield: Approximately ¾ cup
2 tbsp.	raw unfiltered honey, dissolved in 1 tbsp. hot distilled water
2 tbsp.	poppy seeds
½ tsp.	minced onion
1 tsp.	Celtic Sea Salt® (optional)
¼ tsp.	paprika
¼ cup	light oil (sesame or almond)
¼ cup	balsamic vinegar

Place ingredients in a small bowl and whisk to combine well. Refrigerate 1 hour before using.

PAM'S DRESSING

★★★★★	Yield: Approximately 1½ cups
1	large ripe avocado, peeled and pitted
½–1 cup	Tomatillo juice
1–3 cloves	garlic, peeled
	Cayenne pepper to taste (optional)
	Kelp to taste
	Cilantro, basil or parsley to taste (optional)

Place all ingredients in a food processor and process until creamy.

ANITA'S DRESSING
Anita Jones

★	Yield: Approximately 1/3 cup
3 tbsp.	extra virgin cold pressed olive oil
2 tbsp.	Balsamic vinegar (or fresh squeezed lemon juice)
2 tbsp.	fresh squeezed orange juice
	Celtic Sea Salt® to taste (optional)
	Nuts as garnish if desired

Place all ingredients in a shaker jar or small bowl and mix well.

LEMON VINAIGRETTE

★★★★★	Yield: Approximately ¾ cup
½ cup	extra virgin cold pressed olive oil
3 tbsp.	fresh lemon juice
1 tbsp.	fresh thyme (or 1 tsp. dried)
1 tsp.	dill weed
1 tbsp.	fresh chives, chopped
	Celtic Sea Salt® (optional)
	Pinch of cayenne pepper (optional)

Place all ingredients in blender or small jar and blend well.

RASPBERRY VINAIGRETTE

★	
Raspberry syrup base:	
12 oz pkg.	unsweetened frozen raspberries
½ cup	raw unfiltered honey

Place raspberries in a pan over low heat, and warm until thawed. Stir in honey and increase heat, bringing mixture to a rolling boil. Boil for five minutes, stirring constantly. Remove from heat and strain through cheesecloth. After straining, discard raspberries. When syrup has cooled, pour into bottle and refrigerate.

Raspberry Vinaigrette Dressing:	
¾ cup	extra virgin cold pressed olive oil
½ cup	raw unfiltered apple cider vinegar
5 tbsp.	raspberry syrup from recipe above (adjust to taste)
1–2 cloves	garlic, peeled and crushed
	Celtic Sea Salt® to taste (optional)

Place all ingredients in a bowl and whip with a whisk until well blended.

Option: May substitute any berry you prefer.

Note: This dressing recipe can also be found in Salad Dressings for Life … from God's Garden.

Entrees

"And God said, Behold, I have given you every herb bearing seed, which is upon the face of all the earth, and every tree, in the which is the fruit of a tree yielding seed; to you it shall be for meat."

—*Genesis 1:29*

A young boy and his fishing pole—very Tom Sawyer! This is George in 1941, during a Fourth of July at the lake. Here he is fishing for fish, later in life he would become a fisher of men.

You will note that many of the recipes in this section contain only a one-star★ or two-star ★★ rating because they are too rich or they contain ingredients that shouldn't be eaten on a daily basis or they contain ingredients that are too high in fat or protein and should be eaten sparingly. Remember, the one-star★ recipes in this book are to brighten your Holidays and special occasions only. For recipes in keeping with The Hallelujah Diet® for every day, please use the recipes in *Recipes for Life … from God's Garden* and select those recipes that are five-star★★★★★ or four-star★★★★ ratings.This will assist you on your way to *Ultimate Health*. Also, use freely those recipes in this book that are rated with five-star★★ ★★★ or four-star★★★★, unless you want to save them for special occasions.

RAW FETTUCCINE

★★★★★	Serves 2–3
2½–3 cup	zucchini, shredded (or spaghetti squash)
1 small	sweet bell pepper, seeded and sliced into thin strips
½ cup	chives, minced
½ cup	red onion or scallions, diced
½ small	red or yellow bell pepper, seeded and chopped
¼ cup	fresh oregano, minced
¼ cup	fresh basil, minced
2 cloves	garlic, minced
1 small piece	fresh ginger, minced
1 tbsp.	freshly squeezed lemon juice

Process zucchini into "spaghetti" using a shredding blade and processing lengthwise, a potato peeler, or a Spirooli*, and set aside. Place all chopped and shredded ingredients into a bowl and fold in one batch of Pine Nut Cheese (see recipe on page 43).

***Rhonda's Kitchen Tips:** The Spirooli is an inexpensive, practical, and innovative kitchen tool that is safe, fast, and easy to use. One of the blades turns zucchini, beets, potatoes, and other firm vegetables into spaghetti-like strands in just a matter of minutes. The other two blades, which come with this machine, can be used to shred, slice, or dice vegetables and firm fruits. Suction cups on the bottom of the machine quickly attach it to the counter to keep it firmly in place while in operation. The machine is easily cleaned with soap and water, and uses no batteries or electricity. The Spirooli measures 13" L x 9" H.

ORANGE-HERB RICE

★★★	Serves 4
2 tbsp.	onion, chopped fine
2 tbsp.	vegetable soup stock
1 cup	Basmati rice
2 cups	distilled water
½ tsp.	orange zest*
½ cup	fresh orange juice
1 tsp.	Celtic Sea Salt® (optional)
⅛ tsp.	marjoram
⅛ tsp.	thyme

Place all ingredients in a saucepan and bring to a boil, reduce heat to lowest temperature and simmer for 30 minutes. Turn off heat source but do not remover cover for an additional 15 minutes.

Rhonda's Kitchen Tips: Zest is the colored part of the citrus fruit (oranges, lemons, limes, grapefruit, etc.). Use the fine side of a grater or a zesting tool that can be found in kitchen stores.

HOLIDAY CROCK-POT DRESSING
Melanie Bittinger

★★★	Serves 4–6
4 cups	Ezekiel Bread, cubed
2 cups	onions, chopped
2 cups	celery, chopped
1 cup	fresh mushrooms, sliced (optional)
¼ cup	parsley flakes
3 cups	veggie soup stock (see recipe on page 60.)

Place all ingredients in a crock-pot and mix well. Top with ½ cup ground flaxseeds.

Cook on high 45 minutes, then 4–6 hours on low, or cook on high for four hours.

MASHED POTATOES WITH GARLIC

★★★	Serves 6–8
3 lbs.	russet potatoes, peeled and quartered
2 or 3 cloves	garlic, peeled and minced
3 bunches	scallions, cleaned, trimmed, and chopped into ½-inch pieces
1 tsp.	Celtic Sea Salt® (optional)
½ tsp.	Herb Seasoning
1–2 tbsp.	extra virgin cold pressed olive oil

Place potatoes and minced garlic in a saucepan with enough distilled water to cover. Place cover on pan and bring to boil. Reduce heat and cook until fork tender (about 20 minutes). Drain into colander, reserving cooking water.

While potatoes are cooking, wash and chop scallions.

In mixing bowl, mash potatoes using potato masher or electric mixer, adding olive oil and reserved potato water as needed to reach a creamy consistency. Add Celtic Sea Salt® and herb seasonings (to taste). Stir in scallions. Serve with additional olive oil, if desired.

HOLIDAY ACORN SQUASH
Karen C.

★★★	Serves 1–2
1	acorn squash
1 cup	organic raisins
1 cup	organic fresh squeezed orange juice
1 tsp.	cinnamon

Soak raisins in orange juice while preparing and cooking the squash. Cut the squash in half cross-wise. Scoop out and discard strings and seeds. Place cut side down in ½ inch of distilled water in a baking dish. Bake at 375 degrees for 30 minutes, or until tender. Remove squash and drain remaining water. Place half of the soaked raisins with orange juice in each half of squash, sprinkle with cinnamon, cover and return to the oven for approximately 10 more minutes.

PECAN–ONION GRAVY

★★★	*Makes about 6 cups*
3 cups	distilled water
1 medium	onion, chopped
8 tbsp.	oat flour
3 cups	vegetable soup stock (see recipe on p. 60)
1 cup	pecans (or your favorite nut), toasted and finely chopped
1 tsp.	Celtic Sea Salt® (optional)
¼ tsp.	dried thyme
	Herb seasoning to taste
1 cup	mushrooms* (optional)

In a skillet over medium-high heat, brown flour, stirring constantly, until the color is deep amber, about three minutes. Be careful not to burn. Remove from heat and scrape flour onto a plate to cool.

Place onion in skillet and steam sauté until translucent, about three minutes, place in a sauce pan, combine flour with a little soup stock and whisk to combine until smooth. Add remaining soup sock a little at a time whisking to make sure there are no lumps. Add onion, chopped nuts, Celtic Sea Salt®, thyme, and herb seasoning to taste and cook over medium heat, whisking continually until thickened.

*Note: Those who eat mushrooms may add 1 cup mushrooms that have been cleaned and steeped for about 20 minutes in boiling water. The strained soaking water can be used to replace an equal amount of vegetable soup stock.

BAKED CANDIED SWEET POTATOES

★★★	Serves 6–8
8	sweet potatoes (washed but not peeled)
4–6	organic dates, pitted
1 tsp.	Celtic Sea Salt® (optional)
1 tsp.	orange zest*
¼ tsp.	mace
½ tsp.	cinnamon
½ cup	pecans, chopped (or your favorite nut)

Pierce sweet potatoes and bake in 400-degree oven until soft. Remove from oven, place on racks until cool enough to handle.

Cut sweet potatoes in half and scrape potato flesh into large bowl and allow to cool slightly. Puree sweet potatoes and dates in batches in food processor or put through food mill. Pour puree into bowl. Fold in orange zest, seasonings, and nuts. Beat with electric mixer to combine.

Transfer to lecithin** lined ovenproof casserole. Cover dish with plastic wrap and refrigerate until ready for cooking.

To bake, remove from refrigerator and bring to room temperature (about 2 hours). Preheat oven to 350 degrees. Remove plastic wrap. Sprinkle with cinnamon and chopped nuts. Bake until hot, about 30 minutes.

Rhonda's Kitchen Tips: Zest is the colored part of the citrus fruit (oranges, lemons, limes, grapefruit, etc.). Use the fine side of a grater or a zesting tool that can be found in kitchen stores.

****Rhonda's Kitchen Tips:*** Liquid lecithin is a fairly thick pure vegetable product that forms a colloidal solution in water, and has emulsifying, wetting, and antioxidant properties. Place it on a paper towel and "grease" the baking dish, bread pan, or muffin tin, etc. Liquid lecithin is available in health food stores.

SWEET POTATO CASSEROLE
Myra Idol

★	Serves 6
Sweet potatoes:	
3 or 4	sweet potatoes or enough to equal 3 cups
1 tbsp.	pure vanilla extract
½ cup	non-dairy milk substitute
	Pure maple syrup or raw unfiltered honey to taste

Bake sweet potatoes*, cool slightly, peel, and mash. Mix with remaining ingredients. Place in a 1½ quart casserole dish, which has been spread with liquid lecithin**.

*Note: Can prepare sweet potatoes ahead of time, adding topping just before baking.

***Rhonda's Kitchen Tips:** Liquid lecithin is a fairly thick pure vegetable product that forms a colloidal solution in water, and has emulsifying, wetting, and antioxidant properties. Place it on a paper towel and "grease" the baking dish, bread pan, or muffin tin. Liquid lecithin is available in health food stores.

Topping:	

Combine the following and mix well:

1 cup	pure maple syrup
⅓ cup	whole-wheat pastry flour
1 cup	chopped pecans

Spread topping over sweet potatoes and bake 20 minutes at 300 degrees.

GARLIC ROASTED SWEET POTATOES
Becca Brasfield

★	Serves 2–3
The Sweet Potatoes:	
2–3 medium	sweet potatoes, peeled & cut into 1" cubes
1	green organic apple, washed with peel, cut into 1" pieces
4–5 cloves	fresh garlic, diced
2 tbsp.	extra virgin cold pressed olive oil or olive oil spray
Topping:	
1½ tbsp.	date sugar
1½ tbsp.	pecans, chopped
¼ cup	shredded unsweetened coconut
½ tsp.	ginger
½ tsp.	cinnamon
¼ tsp.	Celtic Sea Salt®

Spray a 9" x 13" glass dish with olive oil (or spread with liquid lecithin*). Add potatoes, apple, garlic, and oil and mix well until coated. Bake in a pre-heated oven at 450 degrees for 10 min. then reduce heat to 350 degrees for 30–35 minutes.

Meanwhile, mix topping ingredients together. Remove the casserole from the oven and sprinkle topping mix over them. Let sugar melt a little before serving.

Rhonda's Kitchen Tips: Liquid lecithin is a fairly thick pure vegetable product that forms a colloidal solution in water, and has emulsifying, wetting, and antioxidant properties. Place it on a paper towel and "grease" the baking dish, bread pan, or muffin tin. Liquid lecithin is available in health food stores.

HOLIDAY BREAD STUFFING

★★★	Serves 6–8
8 cups	whole-grain bread, cubed and dried
1½ cups	onion, chopped
2	celery ribs (stalks), chopped
1 cup	mushrooms, sliced (optional)
½ cup	water chestnuts, sliced (optional)
2	sweet apples, peeled and cut into small cubes
1 cup	walnuts or pecans, chopped
1 cup	organic raisins
1 tsp.	sage or to taste
1 tsp.	marjoram or to taste
1 tsp.	thyme or to taste
½ tsp.	Celtic Sea Salt® (optional)
Pinch	cayenne pepper (optional)
2 cups	Vegetable Soup Stock (see recipe on page 60.)
3 tsp.	vegan bouillon powder (or 1 vegan low sodium bouillon cube) (optional)

Place dried bread cubes in a large bowl and set aside. Steam onions, celery and mushrooms (if using) in a small amount of distilled water until onions are transparent. Add sage, marjoram, thyme, sea salt, and cayenne pepper. Mix well and set aside.

Pour Vegetable Soup Stock in Vita-Mix or other blender along with bouillon and process until bouillon is dissolved. Combine ingredients and pour into bread cubes. Toss well until all bread cubes are moistened. (If more liquid is needed additional Vegetable Soup Stock may be used.)

Coat baking dish with liquid lecithin*. Place stuffing in pan (do not pack tightly) and bake at 350 degrees for 30 minutes. For a more moist dressing, cover baking dish.

*Rhonda's Kitchen Tips: Liquid lecithin is a fairly thick pure vegetable product that forms a colloidal solution in water, and has emulsifying, wetting, and antioxidant properties. Place it on a paper towel and "grease" the baking dish, bread pan, or muffin tin. Liquid lecithin is available in health food stores.

WILD RICE DRESSING

★★★	Serves 6–8
4 cups	vegetable soup stock or distilled water (see recipe on page 60.)
¾ cup	Basmati rice or any whole rice that you prefer
¾ cup	Wild Rice
1 medium	onion, chopped
1 pound	fresh mushrooms, cleaned and sliced (optional)
½ cup	fresh parsley, chopped
1 cup	celery, diced
¼ tsp.	sage
⅛ tsp.	marjoram
1 cup	pecan nuts, chopped

Bring soup stock or water to a boil and stir in rices. Lower heat to the lowest temperature, cover and cook until tender about 30 minutes—do NOT lift lid. With cover still in place, turn off heat and allow the pan to sit for another 15 minutes without removing cover.

Add remaining ingredients; stir to mix well. Place in a lecithin* lined casserole, cover, and bake in pre-heated 350-degree oven for about 20 minutes.

Rhonda's Kitchen Tips: Liquid lecithin is a fairly thick pure vegetable product that forms a colloidal solution in water, and has emulsifying, wetting, and antioxidant properties. Place it on a paper towel and "grease" the baking dish, bread pan, or muffin tin. Liquid lecithin is available in health food stores.

LISA WAGNER'S HOLIDAY STUFFING

★	Serves 6–8
3 tbsp.	extra virgin cold pressed olive oil
1 large	onion, chopped
2	celery ribs (stalks), chopped
1 large	carrot, chopped
1 loaf (16 oz)	crusty-type bread, dry, cut into ¼ inch cubes
2½ cups	vegetable soup stock (see recipe on page 60.)
½ tsp.	each: rosemary, thyme, sage,
	Celtic Sea Salt® to taste (optional)
	Pinch of cayenne pepper (or to taste)

In a large saucepan, sauté vegetables in olive oil until tender*. Add bread cubes to saucepan, along with vegetable broth; toss to moisten. Stir in seasonings. Spoon into olive oil-sprayed 9x13 glass pan. Bake at 350 degrees for 35 minutes covered, then uncovered for an additional 10 minutes.

*Option: If ingredients are steam sautéed, this becomes a 3-star (★★★) recipe.

"RAW STUFFING"
Bill & Teresia Cox

★★★★	Serves 2
2 cups	corn cut off the cob
⅓ cup	extra virgin cold pressed olive oil
¼ cup	onion, minced
¼ cup	celery, minced
¼ cup	carrot, shredded
½ cup	lemon juice
1 tsp.	garlic, peeled and minced
1 tsp.	Jalapeño pepper, seeded and minced (optional)
	Celtic Sea Salt® to taste (optional)

Combine the above ingredients in a serving bowl. Mix and serve.

STUFFED TOMATOES

★★★★★	Serves 4
4 large	ripe tomatoes with stems
3 cups	sunflower seeds, soaked overnight and drained
¼ cup	cucumber, chopped
¼ cup	green onions, chopped
¼ cup	ripe red, yellow, or orange bell pepper, seeded and chopped
½ cup	fresh basil, minced
1 clove	garlic, peeled and minced
¼ tsp.	paprika

Cut tops off tomatoes, leaving the stem in place and set aside. Scoop out the pulp and seeds leaving ¼ inch around the outside edge and bottom. Blend sunflower seeds with ½ of the tomato pulp and paprika until smooth. Mix remaining pulp, green onions, bell pepper, basil, and garlic into the blended mixture.

Stuff tomatoes to the top and decorate with your favorite fresh minced herb. Carefully replace tops but be sure they are "stuffed" enough so that the stuffing shows under the lid.

Options: May add fresh corn kernels, shredded carrots, chopped celery, or chopped nuts if not using sunflower seeds.

RAWVIOLI
Top Raw Men

★★★★★	
10	Roma tomatoes, thinly sliced
½ cup	extra virgin cold pressed olive oil
3 cloves	garlic, peeled and minced
1 tsp.	Celtic Sea Salt® (optional)

Combine olive oil, garlic cloves, and sea salt; whisk mix well. Place tomato slices in marinade for at least 15 minutes. While the tomatoes are marinating, prepare the following nut cheese.

NUT CHEESE
Top Raw Men

★★★★★

Prepare by adding the following ingredients into blender and process until creamy:

1 cup	pine nuts*
½ cup	sunflower seeds
½ tbsp.	Celtic Sea Salt® (optional)
¼ cup	fresh basil
2 cloves	garlic, peeled
½ cup	distilled water

Before placing tomatoes on dehydrator screens put a paper towel underneath to catch dripping liquid. Place one tomato slice on dehydrator screen. Add one spoonful of nut cheese on tomato slice. Top with another slice. Repeat until all tomato slices are used. Dehydrate for 8–9 hours at 98 degrees.

Rhonda's Kitchen Tips: Pine nuts (pignoli or pignolia) are the edible, soft, white seed of a number of western North American pine trees. They add versatility in the kitchen with a creamy consistency when used in sauces or dressings and a wonderful texture when used whole. Because pine nuts have a very short shelf life, they should be stored in the freezer.

BAKED BEANS

★	Serves 6–8
2 cups	dried Navy Beans, soaked overnight and drained
4 cups	distilled water
1 medium	onion, chopped
½ cup	pure maple syrup
1½ tsp.	Celtic Sea Salt® (optional)
½ cup	unsulphered molasses (not Blackstrap)
1 tsp.	dry mustard (optional)
1 tsp.	ground ginger
½ tsp.	ground cinnamon

Drain beans and place in a 2-quart saucepan; add 4 cups of distilled water. Bring to a boil over high heat. Cover and reduce heat. Simmer for 2 hours. Drain beans reserving 2 cups of liquid (add additional water to equal 2 cups if necessary).

Preheat oven to 350 degrees. In a small skillet steam sauté onion until onion is translucent. In a lecithin* lined 2-quart baking dish, combine beans, steamed onions, syrup, sea salt, reserved liquid, molasses, mustard, ginger, and cinnamon. Mix well. Cover and bake 2 hours, stirring occasionally. Add more water if necessary. Uncover and bake 35 to 45 minutes or until the top is browned.

***Rhonda's Kitchen Tips:** Liquid lecithin is a fairly thick pure vegetable product that forms a colloidal solution in water, and has emulsifying, wetting, and antioxidant properties. Place it on a paper towel and "grease" the baking dish, bread pan, or muffin tin. Liquid lecithin is available in health food stores.

VEGETARIAN POT PIE

★	Serves 6–8
Dough:	
1½ cups	spelt flour
1 cup	whole-wheat pastry or oat flour
¼ cup	rolled oats (coarsely chopped in food processor using the "S" blade)
1 tsp.	Celtic Sea Salt® (optional)
½ cup	grape seed oil
⅔ cup	non-dairy milk

Mix all dry ingredients together. In a separate bowl, combine milk and oil; add dry ingredients. Mix slowly. Dough should be soft and pliable. If it is too dry, add a little more liquid.

Filling:	
1 medium	carrot, diced
1	celery rib (stalk) , diced
1 large	onion, chopped
2 medium	potatoes, diced
1 cup	frozen peas
1 cup	frozen corn
2 tbsp.	whole-wheat pastry or oat flour
1 cup	distilled water
½ tsp.	Celtic Sea Salt® (optional)
1 tbsp.	grape seed oil
2 tbsp.	baby oats
2 tbsp.	All Purpose seasoning
2	bay leaves (optional)

Lightly steam carrot, potatoes, celery, and onion until tender. Add peas and corn and set aside. Place flour and oats in a skillet and heat slowly to brown slightly. Add water whisking as it is added to prevent lumping. Add seasonings and bay leaves. Continue cooking until mixture has thickened. Remove bay leaves. Add vegetables and mix well to coat.

Preheat oven to 350 degrees. Roll out half of the dough to ⅛ inch thick and place in pie plate. Carefully add filling. Roll out the remainder of the dough and place on top; crimp edges. Bake for about 30 minutes, until edges are slightly brown.

SQUASH SUPREME

★★★	Serves 6
6 cups	winter squash, peeled and chopped
½ cup	onion, chopped
3 cups	tomatoes, peeled and chopped
⅔ cup	celery, chopped
½ tsp.	parsley, minced
⅛ tsp.	dried basil, minced
⅛ tsp.	Italian seasoning (optional)
	Herb seasoning as desired

Dry roast onion over low heat until translucent and slightly browned in a large skillet. Add remaining ingredients and cover and simmer for about 25 minutes or until squash is soft. Serve with a nice salad and fresh homemade bread.

HOLIDAY SWEET POTATOES
Mary Ann Slaughter

★★	Serves 4
4	sweet potatoes
1 tsp.	cinnamon (or to taste)
	Juice of one organic orange
¼	fresh pineapple, peeled and cut into bite size pieces
¾ cup	pecans, chopped

Bake sweet potatoes in a 350-degree oven until tender. Cool slightly and remove skins. Mash with cinnamon adding fresh squeezed orange juice, if liquid is needed. Place into casseole. Top with fresh pineapple chunks and pecans. Bake at 350-degrees until topping starts to brown.

RAW "BURRITOS"

★★★★★	Serves 2
¼ cup	fresh mint, (peppermint, spearmint, or your choice), minced
2 cups	ripe avocado, peeled, pitted, and diced
½	small ripe tomato, finely chopped
2	scallions, minced, or 2 tbsp. red onion, finely chopped
1 tbsp.	sweet bell pepper, seeded and finely chopped
½ tsp.	Celtic Sea Salt® (optional)
1 tbsp.	fresh cilantro, minced, or ½ tsp. dried
½ tsp.	cumin
½ tsp.	powdered kelp (optional)
¼ cup	lemon or lime juice
4 large	Napa Cabbage leaves (or Romaine lettuce) leaves

Mix all but cabbage or romaine in a bowl. To make Burritos spoon equal portions of the avocado mixture into the cabbage (or lettuce) leaves. Wrap around the mixture, secure with a toothpick and serve with a raw soup.

GARDEN CASSEROLE

★	Serves 4–5
1 cup	potatoes, diced (about 1 medium potato)
1 cup	zucchini squash, diced (about 1 medium zucchini)
1 cup	carrots, diced (I large or 3 medium carrots)
1 cup	fresh or frozen corn kernels
1 cup	fresh or frozen peas
½ cup	red onion, diced (about 1 medium onion)
1 cup	distilled water
¼ cup	oat flour
¼ tsp.	ground celery seed
1 tsp.	Celtic Sea Salt® (optional)
Pinch	cayenne pepper (optional)
2 cups	non-dairy milk
¼ cup	non-dairy shredded cheddar cheese (optional)
¼ cup	whole-grain bread crumbs, dry roasted in skillet or ground whole-grain cracker crumbs

Preheat oven to 400 degrees. Place vegetables in a large skillet and steam sauté until just tender; drain. Reduce heat to medium and return to skillet. Sprinkle flour over vegetables; stir to blend. Combine next 6 ingredients using a wire whisk. Pour slowly over the vegetables and cook 10 to 15 minutes, stirring occasionally, until thick. Pour into lecithin* lined 9-inch glass pie plate. Sprinkle with non-dairy cheddar and bread crumbs. Bake 15 to 20 minutes or until bubbly.

*__Rhonda's Kitchen Tips:__ Liquid lecithin is a fairly thick pure vegetable product that forms a colloidal solution in water, and has emulsifying, wetting, and antioxidant properties. Place it on a paper towel and "grease" the baking dish, bread pan, or muffin tin. Liquid lecithin is available in health food stores.

HOLIDAY SWEET POTATO SOUFFLÉ
Addy Glenna

★	Serves 4
4	sweet potatoes, peeled and cut into chunks
1	orange, juiced
2–3 tbsp.	raw unfiltered honey (or to taste)
¼ cup	almond milk or rice milk
2–3 tbsp.	maple syrup (for topping)

Boil sweet potatoes until soft. Mash them and add the orange juice, honey, and milk. Mix thoroughly and put in a liquid lecithin* lined casserole dish. Drizzle maple syrup over the top and bake for about 30 minutes at 350 degrees or until heated through.

Rhonda's Kitchen Tips: Liquid lecithin is a fairly thick pure vegetable product that forms a colloidal solution in water, and has emulsifying, wetting, and antioxidant properties. Place it on a paper towel and "grease" the baking dish, bread pan, or muffin tin. Liquid lecithin is available in health food stores.

BROWN RISOTTO
Mary Ann Street

★	Serves 4
2 tbsp.	extra virgin cold pressed olive oil
1 small	onion, chopped
1 cup	brown rice
2½ cups	distilled water
1 tsp.	vegetable bouillon
	Salt substitute to taste

Sauté the onion in olive oil until softened. Add the rice, then liquid, and seasonings. Cover the pan and cook over med-low heat for about 45 minutes, until liquid is absorbed.

RAW LASAGNA

★★★★★ | **Serves 8–10**

Lasagna was one of the favorite dishes we served at our restaurant. I've since learned to make it raw. The texture and taste will be different from what you may be used to, but allow your taste buds the opportunity to learn to appreciate the wonderful bounty and taste sensations from God's magnificent creation! Who knows, you may start a whole new tradition in your family!

To prepare this recipe you will need to have made the Basic Marinade found on page 44, the Raw Italian Sauce found on page 39 and Macadamia Pine Nut Cheese on page 55.

4	zucchini, sliced lengthwise in very thin strips
2–3 cups	fresh spinach, washed and drained
1	red sweet bell pepper, seeded and sliced into thin strips or chopped
1 bunch	scallions, chopped (or 1 sweet red onion)
3–4 large	ripe tomatoes, sliced very thin

After preparing the vegetables marinade them in the Basic Marinade for about for four hours. Mix well to make sure all of the vegetables are well coated. Drain well when ready to assemble Lasagna.

This dish will be made in layers so make sure you use only a portion of the ingredients in each layer. In a 9" x 12" glass cake pan place a thin layer of Raw Italian Sauce. Add a layer of well drained zucchini "noodles," top with spinach, bell peppers, scallions, and sliced tomatoes. Carefully top with Macadamia Pine Nut Cheese. Repeat layers ending with a layer of sliced tomatoes, Raw Italian Sauce, and a bit of the Macadamia Pine Nut Cheese. May sprinkle a few ground macadamia nuts on top, if desired or crumbled Macadamia Pine Nut Cheese that has been dehydrated until dry (see page 55). Cover with plastic wrap and allow the flavors to marry at room temperature until ready to serve.

May warm in dehydrator, if desired.

PASTA WITH BROCCOLI
AND PINE NUTS

★★★	Serves 4–6
8 ounces	spinach pasta (fettuccini, angel hair, etc.)
2 cups	broccoli florets and stems
2 cloves	garlic, peeled and minced
2 tbsp.	pine nuts* (or pecans, almonds, etc.)
3 cups	tomato, chopped
1 tbsp.	extra virgin cold pressed olive oil
	Celtic Sea Salt® to taste (optional)
	Pinch of cayenne pepper or to taste (optional)

In a large pot bring water to boil and cook pasta until tender. Break broccoli into florets and slice tender stems into thin rounds. In a large pan combine broccoli, ½ cup tomatoes, pine nuts, and garlic and steam over low to medium heat for 5 to 10 minutes (add a small amount of distilled water if necessary). Remove from heat and add the rest of the tomatoes, olive oil, and seasonings.

Serve over cooked pasta and enjoy! Makes a nice meal when served with a crisp green salad.

*__Rhonda's Kitchen Tips:__ Pine nuts (pignoli or pignolia) are the edible, soft, white seed of a number of western North American pine trees. They add versatility in the kitchen with a creamy consistency when used in sauces or dressings and a wonderful texture when used whole. Because pine nuts have a very short shelf life, they should be stored in the freezer.

RAW ZUCCHINI PASTA

★★★★★

Process zucchini into "pasta" by using a Spirooli* to spiral slice or by using a food processor where the shredding blade has been inserted. Place zucchini lengthwise in a food processor and run the machine creating long strands of zucchini pasta. It has a similar texture and taste to angel hair pasta. "Noodles" may be warmed in a dehydrator or in warm, but not boiling, water. Top "pasta" with any of the following sauces:

Barbeque Sauce, page 41
Raw Italian Sauce, page 39
Alla Checca Sauce, page 42
Basic Pesto Sauce, page 48
Guacamole Sauce, page 44

__Rhonda's Kitchen Tips:__ The Spirooli is an inexpensive, practical, and innovative kitchen tool that is safe, fast, and easy to use. One of the blades turns zucchini, beets, potatoes, and other firm vegetables into spaghetti-like strands in just a matter of minutes. The other two blades, which come with this machine, can be used to shred, slice, or dice vegetables and firm fruits. Suction cups on the bottom of the machine quickly attach it to the counter to keep it firmly in place while in operation. The machine is easily cleaned with soap and water, and uses no batteries or electricity. The Spirooli measures 13" L x 9" H.

SAFFRON RICE
Mary Ann Street

★	Serves 4
3 tbsp.	extra virgin cold pressed olive oil
1 small	onion, chopped
3 cloves	garlic, minced
3 cups	vegetable soup stock (see page 60)
½ tsp.	saffron*, crumbled
1½ cups	Basmati rice
	Salt substitute to taste

Heat oil in large casserole and sauté onion and garlic until onion is soft. Add soup stock and saffron and bring to a boil. Stir in the rice and salt substitute. Cook over medium-high heat, uncovered, for about 10 minutes or until rice is semi-dry but some liquid remains. Cover and cook over low heat for about 20 minutes. Turn rice over with a fork, from bottom to top, then cover and cook for about 10 more minutes.

*Note: See Saffron in the Herb Listing in the Glossary of Ingredients.

BURGERS AND GRAVY OVER RICE
Pamela Eskridge

★	Serves 4–6
4–6	frozen veggie burgers (your own burgers or those purchased at a local health food store)
1 large	onion, peeled
2–3 cups	non-dairy milk
	Celtic Sea Salt® to taste (optional)
1 tsp.	onion powder or to taste
1 tbsp.	arrowroot powder mixed in enough distilled water to dissolve

Steam sauté onions in a little water until slightly translucent, add veggie burgers and cook until heated through and browned. Remove burgers when browned and set aside. In the pan with the onions, add non-dairy milk and seasonings and mix well. Stir in arrowroot powder mixture and whisk until a thick gravy is obtained. Return burgers to pan, simmer a few minutes, and serve over prepared Basmati rice.

"CREAMED" CAULIFLOWER

★★★★★	Serves 2–4
1 small head or ½ large head	cauliflower
¾ cup	pine nuts*, soaked overnight and drained
¼ cup	macadamia nuts, soaked overnight and drained
⅓ cup	distilled water or soaking water from nuts
2 tbsp.	extra virgin cold pressed olive oil
3 tbsp.	fresh lemon juice
1 tbsp.	onion, minced
¼ tsp.	thyme
¼ tsp.	poultry seasoning
½ tsp.	Celtic Sea Salt® (optional)

Cut cauliflower into pieces. Process all other ingredients until creamy. Add cauliflower a little at a time and process until smooth. May top with chopped green onions or chives to add color.

*__Rhonda's Kitchen Tips:__ Pine nuts (pignoli or pignolia) are the edible, soft, white seed of a number of western North American pine trees. They add versatility in the kitchen with a creamy consistency when used in sauces or dressings and a wonderful texture when used whole. Because pine nuts have a very short shelf life, they should be stored in the freezer.

BETTER THAN "TUNA"

| ★★★★★ | *Serves 2–4* |

This recipe is also found in *Recipes for Life … from God's Garden* and is one so many people have told me they love so I am including it in this book as well.

2 cups	carrots, shredded
1 medium	red bell pepper, seeded and chopped
1 medium	ripe tomato, chopped (optional)
2	celery ribs (stalks), chopped fine
½ medium	red onion, chopped fine
½ cup	fresh parsley, minced
½ tsp.	kelp
½ tsp.	Celtic Sea Salt® (optional)
4 tbsp.	Rhonda's No-Oil Salad Dressing (see Recipes for Life … from God's Garden)

Place vegetables in bowl and combine dressing with seasonings. Mix well and allow flavors to mingle. May serve on a bed of dark green lettuce (not iceberg) or mixed greens, in a sandwich, pita pocket, or used to stuff tomatoes or cucumber boats.

Option: Vegenaise® may be used instead of Rhonda's No-Oil Salad Dressing, but the recipe becomes a 1-star (★).

Option: Omit dressing and add ½ cup sunflower seeds, soaked overnight and drained, ½ cup macadamia nuts, soaked overnight and drained. Top with grated carrot, chopped scallions, or minced fresh parsley.

MEXICAN RICE

B. J. Menikos

★	Serves 4
	Extra virgin cold pressed olive oil
½ large	onion, diced
1 medium	Poblano pepper, diced (optional)
2 cups	brown rice
4 tbsp.	tomato puree + water to make 4 cups of liquid
1 15 oz. can	diced tomatoes
½ cup	frozen corn
½ cup	cooked beans, drained and rinsed (red or black work best)
1 tsp.	chili powder (optional)
½ tsp.	garlic powder
1 tsp.	cumin

Put olive oil in a deep saucepan and brown the brown rice in it, along with the onion and Poblano pepper. Add the remaining ingredients and bring to a boil. Reduce heat, cover pan, and cook for 40–45 minutes.

Option: If ingredients are steam sautéed, this becomes a 3-star (★★★) recipe.

RICE PILAF WITH CHICK PEAS
Jan Baxter

★	Serves 2–3
2 tbsp.	non-dairy butter or oil
1	onion, chopped
½ tsp.	ground cumin or curry powder
1 cup	long grain wild rice (or combination)
2 cups	vegetable soup stock (see recipe on page 60) or distilled water
19 oz. can	chickpeas, rinsed and well drained
1	green onion, chopped
	Season to taste

Heat butter or oil in medium sized saucepan. Add onion, cook until tender, about 5 minutes. Add cumin or curry powder. Cook another 30 seconds just to release flavor. Stir in rice, coat well. Add stock or water. Bring to boil. Reduce heat, cover, and simmer gently 15 minutes. Add chickpeas; cook 10 minutes longer until all the liquid has been absorbed. Stir in green onion. Add seasonings to taste, and butter if using. Makes 4 servings.

Option: If ingredients are steam sautéed, this becomes a 3-star (★★★) recipe.

WILD RICE, CARROTS, AND MUSHROOMS
Linda Mullen

★	Serves 2
1	onion, chopped
½–1 cup	celery, chopped
Handful	mushrooms, chopped (optional)
3–4	carrots, grated
1 cup	Lundberg Wild Rice Blend
½–1 tsp.	Celtic Sea Salt® (optional)
1 tbsp.	Frontier™ All-Purpose Seasoning
1 tbsp.	extra virgin cold pressed olive oil

Cook wild rice according to package directions with all-purpose seasoning added to water. Sauté onions, celery, and mushrooms (if using) in olive oil until tender along with Celtic Sea Salt®. Stir wild rice and grated carrots together with the sautéed vegetables. Cook only until the mixture is heated through.

Option: If ingredients are steam sautéed, this becomes a 3-star (★★★) recipe.

RAGIN' CAJUN BEANS AND RICE
Arnold Pancratz

★★★	Serves 3–4
2 cups	cooked Basmati rice
1 1-pound can	salt-free diced tomatoes
1 cup	onion, diced
½ cup	bell pepper, seeded and diced
1 1-pound can	red beans
1 tsp.	garlic powder
½ tsp.	cayenne pepper (optional)

I mix my onions, pepper, garlic powder, and cayenne pepper with dry rice before cooking it. I prefer using my rice steamer, but use your preferred method of cooking it if you don't own a steamer. After rice mixture is cooked, mix with other ingredients and serve.

VEGGIE WRAPS
Top Raw Men

★★★★★

The Pâté:

Place the "S" blade in a food processor and add the following:

¼ cup	red cabbage
2 cup	spelt, soaked in 3 cups of distilled water for 8 hours, strain and discard water
2 tbsp.	extra virgin cold pressed olive oil
3 tbsp.	fresh lemon juice
1 tsp.	Celtic Sea Salt® (optional)

When all ingredients have been added, turn on machine and process for 30 seconds or until it is smooth like pâté.

Mixed Vegetables:

In a bowl add:

1 cup	cauliflower, chopped
1 cup	broccoli, chopped
2 tbsp.	extra virgin cold pressed olive oil
2 tsp.	paprika
	Celtic Sea Salt® to taste (optional)

Mix well. Spread the pâté on a red chard leaf and top with mixed vegetables. Roll and enjoy.

STUFFED EGGPLANT
"The Waites"

★	Serves 3–4

When I was in Germany some years ago, I had a wonderful eggplant dish. I asked the waitress in my halting German if I could talk to the chef. He wrote out his recipe and here it is.

2 cups	brown rice
1 large	eggplant
3 tbsp.	extra virgin cold pressed olive oil
1 medium	onion, chopped
1 clove	garlic, minced
2	fresh tomatoes, chopped

Cook 2 cups brown rice in 4 cups water. While rice is cooking:

Slice a large eggplant in half lengthwise and cut the flesh out leaving ½ inch along the sides and bottom of the eggplant. Cube the eggplant that has been removed from the skin and sauté in olive oil with chopped onion and minced garlic. Add chopped tomatoes and sauté further. Turn heat to lowest setting, cover, and cook for 5 minutes. Combine with the brown rice. Pile this mixture atop the halved eggplant and bake in a 350-degree oven for 30 minutes.

Option: If ingredients are steam sautéed, this becomes a 3-star (★★★) recipe.

EGGPLANT AND PASTA
Linda Bingham

★	Serves 2
1	eggplant
1 small jar	pine nuts*
1	yellow bell pepper, seeded
1	red bell pepper, seeded
	Broccoli floretts (or frozen broccoli, thawed)
	Roma tomatoes
	Sun-dried or dehydrated tomatoes (optional)
1 can	small pitted black olives
	Italian seasoning (to taste)
	garlic powder (to taste)
	Celtic Sea Salt® (optional)
1 12 oz.–16 oz. package	vegetable flavored spirals or rotini
	Non-dairy Parmesan Cheese (optional)

Preheat the oven to 400 degrees (or you might try to broil to get the roasted flavor). Take a nice eggplant, halve it lengthwise, and slice it into thin pieces. Brush some olive oil on both sides of the pieces. Sprinkle it with garlic powder and Italian seasoning. You want it to brown on both sides and the peel to become a little leathery.

While the eggplant roasts, wash and slice one yellow bell pepper and one red-orange bell pepper. Also, separate the tops of young broccoli (or get the prepackaged broccoli floretts). Now take your steamer basket and steam the broccoli until tender; do not overcook. Add the peppers to the steamer after the broccoli is tender so the zest of pepper does not overwhelm the broccoli.

While the peppers and broccoli are steaming, boil the pasta and slice some fresh tomatoes. Have on hand the small black-pitted olives and the small jar of pine nuts. (Periodically check the eggplant so that it does not burn to a crisp.) Cook pasta—until just tender, not overcooked.

Drain pasta. Add a small capful or two of olive oil so that the pasta glides smoothly when other ingredients are folded into it. Fold in the steamed veggies and gently mix with wooden spatula. Fold in the eggplant. Mix. Fold in the pine nuts. Mix. Fold in the tomatoes and olives. Season with garlic powder, and add Celtic Sea Salt® and Parmesan Cheese to taste. Serve as a warm dish.

Options: If Parmesan Cheese is omitted, this becomes a 2-star (★★) recipe. If Parmesan Cheese and olives are omitted, this becomes a 3-star (★★★) recipe.

***Rhonda's Kitchen Tips:** Pine nuts (pignoli or pignolia) are the edible, soft, white seed of a number of western North American pine trees. They add versatility in the kitchen with a creamy consistency when used in sauces or dressings and a wonderful texture when used whole. Because pine nuts have a very short shelf life, they should be stored in the freezer.

RA TA TUI
Andrea J. Monroe

★★★	Serves 2
1 cup	Basmati brown rice
1	eggplant, cubed
1	cucumber, cubed
1	zucchini, cubed
1	green bell pepper, seeded and cubed
1	yellow or red bell pepper, seeded and cubed
	Mushrooms, cubed (optional)
1	onion, chopped
2	tomatoes
	Celtic Sea Salt® (optional)
	cumin, to taste
1 clove	garlic, peeled and minced
	oregano, to taste

Steam Basmati rice for 60 minutes. Meanwhile, cube eggplant, cucumber, zucchini, bell peppers, and mushrooms (if using). Chop onion.

Steam veggies and the tomatoes (steam whole) for 20 minutes. Peel the skin off tomatoes. Blend all ingredients. Add Celtic Sea Salt® and spices to taste.

4-VEGGIE GINGER STIR FRY
Mark Kutolowski

★	Serves 1 meal per day

Hi! Being a single 23-year-old and often rushed or eating alone, simplicity is a high priority for me. If I cut up a bunch of the vegetables in this dish at the beginning of the week, I can have dinner ready in 10 minutes each day! Here it is:

Equal proportions of 4 vegetables, cut into bite sized pieces:

Broccoli florets
Snow peas (or other peas in pods)
Mushrooms (optional)
Eggplant (peeled)
Extra virgin cold pressed olive oil
Fresh ginger, minced (or powdered)
Celtic Sea Salt® (optional)
Brown rice base

Lightly cover the face of a skillet with olive oil and heat until water sizzles when dropped on it. Add the broccoli florets and the snow peas, and stir-fry them until crisp but tender, adding ginger and Celtic Sea Salt® to taste. When crisp but tender, add mushrooms (if using) and eggplant. Remove when the eggplant is browned and soft—usually only a few minutes. Serve the stir-fry over brown rice, and enjoy!

VEGGIES AND RICE
Roxanna Ferris

★★★	

Here's one of my favorite meals. Very simple and easy to make; can make a lot or a little, to suit your needs. I make it this way:

Cook brown rice (or whatever kind you want).

When the rice is done cooking, turn off the heat and add small, chopped, UNCOOKED veggies, such as broccoli, carrot, celery, and bell pepper or your favorite. Stir to warm the veggies, but not cook them. Add seasonings (herbs, etc.), and Celtic Sea Salt®. Enjoy!

CROCK-POT PILAF

| ★ | *Serves 2–3* |

This pilaf recipe is for a four-quart Crock-pot; if using a two-quart Crock-pot, reduce the recipe by half.

2½ cups	distilled water (or vegetable soup stock, page 60)
16 ounces	tomatoes, peeled and chopped (or salt-free tomato sauce)
1	medium ripe bell pepper, seeded and chopped
1 large clove	garlic (or two small), peeled and minced (optional)
1 medium	onion, chopped
⅔ cup	ripe black olives*, sliced and rinsed (optional)
1½ cups	raw (uncooked) organic Basmati rice
2 tsp.	All Purpose seasoning
¼ tsp.	Celtic Sea Salt® (optional)

Place all ingredients in the Crock-pot and stir well. Cover and cook on low 6 to 9 hours or on high 3 hours.

Serve with your favorite salad for a hearty meal.

*Option: If olives are omitted, this becomes a 3-star (★★★) recipe.

FESTIVE PEPPERS AND SQUASH
Helen Brownell

★★★	Serves 6–8
2 cups	raw brown rice (or a blend of brown and wild rices)
4 cups	distilled water
¼ tsp.	Celtic Sea Salt® (optional)
½ tsp.	dried garlic
1 tbsp.	dried onion

Boil the distilled water and add seasonings, add rice and bring the mixture back to a rolling boil with the lid off for 5 minutes. Turn the stove down to simmer and place the lid on with vent open. Simmer 30 minutes without peeking, turn burner off, and allow to set 15 minutes.

While the rice is cooking place ¼ cup distilled water in saucepan and steam until barely tender:

2 large	carrots sliced
4 cups	butternut squash cut in small chunks
	Sprinkling of dehydrated garlic and onions
When barely tender add:	
½	green pepper, seeded and sliced
½	red or yellow pepper, seeded and sliced
1	crookneck squash, cut in small chunks
1 medium	zucchini, sliced

Just before removing from the heat, sprinkle with freshly minced parsley or chopped basil. Mix well to combine rice and vegetable mixture. Remove from heat and serve immediately.

FRESH LINGUINI WITH
SUN BAKED TOMATO SAUCE
Audrey McKinnon

★	**Serves 4–6**

The sauce "cooks" on the windowsill! The simple flavors of these simple fresh ingredients combine and blend in the sun before being tossed with fresh pasta.

3 cups	cherry tomatoes, halved
1 large	red onion, sliced very thin
3 large cloves	garlic, minced
⅓ cup	flat leaf parsley, chopped
1½ cups	fresh basil, chopped
1½ tbsp.	balsamic vinegar
⅓ cup	fruity extra virgin cold pressed olive oil
12 ounces	fresh linguini pasta
⅓ cup	pitted Greek or Sicilian olives (optional)
½ cup	grated Asiago cheese (optional)
	Celtic Sea Salt® (optional)
Pinch	cayenne pepper (optional)

In a large shallow non-metallic pan, combine tomatoes, onion, garlic, parsley and 1 cup of the basil. Toss with balsamic vinegar and oil. Cover loosely with waxed paper. Place pan on a hot sunny window ledge for 4 to 6 hours, stir, then add salt and pepper to taste.

Cook pasta in lightly salted boiling water until done al dente. Drain. Add sun baked tomato mixture and the remaining 1/2 cup basil, tossing until combined. Sprinkle with olives and cheese before serving, adding salt and cayenne pepper to taste. Serve warm or at room temperature.

Note: Omit the olives and cheese and this becomes a 5-star (★★★★★) recipe.

"CRAB" DELIGHT
Missy Dawson

★★★★★	Serves 4–6

This recipe is from *Living in the Raw* by Rose Lee Calabro and receives rave reviews from both raw fooders and cooked fooders alike. It is perfect to go with a lunch or dinner salad and gives the meal a feeling of substance. Umm, Umm, Good!

3 cups	almonds, soaked 12–18 hours
3	celery ribs (stalks), finely chopped
1	red bell pepper, seeded and finely chopped
½	red onion, finely chopped
2 tbsp.	fresh lemon juice
½ tsp.	Celtic Sea Salt® (optional)
1–2 tsp.	kelp powder (optional, but this is what gives this dish its fishy flavor)

Process soaked almonds through a Champion or Green Life juicer using the solid blank. Be sure to put the catch basin at the end of the snout. (You could also use a food processor with the "S" blade, but this doesn't get the almonds as creamy). Add remaining ingredients and mix well.

BETTER THAN SAUSAGE

★★★★★	Serves 8
1 cup	pumpkin seeds, soaked overnight, drained and dehydrated
Handful	dark leafy greens
½ cup	extra virgin olive oil
4 cloves	garlic, peeled
½ cup	dehydrated onion flakes
1 Tbsp.	caraway seeds
¼ cup	fresh sage or 1 Tbsp. dried
½ cup	fresh basil or 2 tsp. dried

Blend all ingredients in a food processor using an S blade. Form into patties and serve as is or place in dehydrator at under 105 degrees on a mesh screen and dry for 4 – 8 hours.

RAW CARIBBEAN WILD RICE

★	Serves 2–4
1 cup	wild rice, soaked 48 hours and drained
1	medium onion, chopped (Vidalia's are great in season or a red onion works well)
2 large	tomatoes or 3 medium, chopped
2 large	red bell peppers, seeded and chopped
2 large	yellow bell peppers, seeded and chopped
1–1½ cups	freshly grated coconut
⅔ cup	non-dairy milk
2 tsp.	chili powder (optional)
1–4 cloves	garlic, peeled and pressed or minced
2 tsp.	ground coriander
1 tsp.	ground mustard (optional)
1–2 tsp.	lime zest (use only organic limes)
1	lime, juiced
	Celtic Sea Salt® to taste (optional)

Combine all ingredients in a large bowl and mix well. Keeps for 2–3 days in the refrigerator if covered tightly.

Note: The non-dairy milk makes this a 1-star (★) recipe. If you use almond milk , the recipe becomes a 5-star (★★★★★).

BAKED ACORN SQUASH WITH APPLES
Pikol

★	Serves 2
1	Acorn Squash
5	sweet apples
1 cup	organic raisins
1 cup	chopped English walnuts
2 tsp.	cinnamon or as desired
	A dollop of raw unfiltered honey
	Distilled water

Cut Acorn Squash in half, remove seeds, and place in baking dish with opened cut side facing the bottom of the dish. Put about 2 inches of distilled water in the pan. Bake in 350-degree oven for about 1 hour or until fork tender. Remove from oven and set aside.

Cut up apples and place in a saucepan with remaining ingredients. Heat and stir until the mixture is soft and the aroma is fragrant. Shut off heat. When the Acorn Squash is soft and cool enough to handle, scoop out the squash. You may want to cut in chunks or use a melon ball scoop, what ever works for you, and mix with the apple mixture. Serve it warm as a dinner dish or chilled as dessert; either way, people want more.

Option: Replace honey with 1–2 soaked, pitted, and pureed dates and this becomes a 3-star (★★★) recipe.

Option: Add a little fresh shredded coconut and ginger!

LINGUINI WITH PESTO

★★★

Cook the pasta* until tender. While pasta is cooking, prepare one batch of Basic Pesto found on page 48. Drain pasta when it has finished cooking and fold pesto sauce into it. Mix well and serve with a garden salad.

*Option: For a raw dish, this recipe may be made using the Spirooli** to make zucchini spaghetti instead of using grain pasta. If using this raw dish option, this becomes a 5-star (★★★★★) recipe.

Rhonda's Kitchen Tips: The Spirooli is an inexpensive, practical, and innovative kitchen tool that is safe, fast, and easy to use. One of the blades turns zucchini, beets, potatoes, and other firm vegetables into spaghetti-like strands in just a matter of minutes. The other two blades, which come with this machine, can be used to shred, slice, or dice vegetables and firm fruits. Suction cups on the bottom of the machine quickly attach it to the counter to keep it firmly in place while in operation. The machine is easily cleaned with soap and water, and uses no batteries or electricity. The Spirooli measures 13" L x 9" H.

AVOCADO BURRITO

★★★★★	Serves 4
2	ripe avocados
2 small	bell peppers, minced
4 medium	ripe tomatoes, chopped
⅛ cup	carrot, finely shredded
1 clove	garlic, peeled and minced
1	orange, juiced
8 leaves	dark green lettuce

In a medium bowl, mash avocados and fold in peppers, tomatoes and carrots and garlic. Squeeze orange juice over the top. Equally divide mixture between leaves and roll up like a burrito.

Option: May serve with salsa.

PAT'S PECAN AND RICE PATTIES
Pat Walker

★★★	Serves 4–6
1 cup	pecans, chopped
1 cup	brown rice, cooked
1 cup	fresh whole-grain bread crumbs
1 to 2 tbsp.	whole-grain flour
2	celery ribs (stalks), chopped
1 to 2 tbsp.	parsley, chopped
1 small	onion, finely chopped
1 cup	distilled water

Combine all ingredients and shape into 3-inch patties. Place on cookie sheet that has been sprayed with liquid lecithin*. Bake in a 350-degree pre-heated oven for about 40–45 minutes, or until golden brown.

Rhonda's Kitchen Tips: Liquid lecithin is a fairly thick pure vegetable product that forms a colloidal solution in water, and has emulsifying, wetting, and antioxidant properties. Place it on a paper towel and "grease" the baking dish, bread pan, or muffin tin, etc. Liquid lecithin is available in health food stores.

VEGETABLE PATE

★★★★★	Serves 6–8
1 small	head cauliflower, cut into large pieces
1 small	red or yellow bell pepper, seeded and quartered
1 small	yellow squash, sliced in large circles
1 small	zucchini squash, sliced in large circles
1 cup	sunflower seeds, soaked and drained
¼–½	red onion, chopped fine
¼–½ cup	parsley leaves with stems removed
1 cup	mixed vegetables (may used dehydrated)
½ tsp.	garlic, peeled and minced
¼ cup	green onions or shallots, chopped
⅓ cup	ground flaxseeds*
2–3 tsp.	flaxseed oil
¾ tsp.	ground cumin
½ tsp.	curry powder
½ tsp.	ground coriander
	Pinch of Celtic Sea Salt® (optional)

Replace screen with the blank in Champion or Green Star Juicer. Place a large bowl under the snout end. Process cauliflower, red bell pepper, squash, sunflower seeds, red onion, and parsley through the machine. Run the mixture through a second time. Stir in mixed vegetables, minced garlic, green onion, ground flaxseeds, oil, and seasonings. Mix well. Refrigerate the pate for at least 1 hour. Stir the mixture, taste and adjust for seasoning. Mold into desired shape, cover with plastic wrap and keep refrigerated.

*__Rhonda's Kitchen Tips:__ To grind flaxseeds, place them in a clean electric coffee grinder and grind until powder consistency is reached.

Breads

*"Take thou also unto thee wheat, and barley, and beans,
and lentiles, and millet, and fitches, and put them in one vessel,
and make thee bread thereof...."*

—Ezekiel 4:9

---

*At 21, I had come a long way from my childhood "cake incident!" In this
picture I'm serving at an Easter luncheon. Without knowing it, I was
beginning the journey that would fulfill God's destiny for me.*

A Word About Whole-Grain Flours
and Bread Baking

We are often told that bread made with organic whole-grain flours are too heavy and that unbleached flour needs to be added to lighten the loaf. When using store bought whole-grain flours, this is usually true. However, when using a grain mill to process the whole grains (millet, flax, spelt, oats, barley, quinoa, kamut, rye, or other whole grains) into flour, the bread turns out much lighter than when made with purchased whole-grain flours. Another plus for grinding your own grains and baking your own homemade breads is that you control and know exactly what ingredients have been used.

You will note that in the above list, whole-wheat flour is absent. We try to avoid using a great deal of whole-wheat flour, because it is one of the most acidic of all of the grains, and the gluten it contains may also be a problem. Thus, we consider it one of the poorer grains to consume and it should not be eaten on a daily basis. In the following recipes, any other whole-grain flour may be substituted for the whole-wheat, if you so desire. You might like to try quinoa, spelt, rice, or oat flour instead; however, the texture may be slightly different.

It is interesting to note that breads are much higher on the glycemic index than carrot juice and invoke a greater insulin response. When farmers want to fatten cattle, they put them on grain. For this reason as well, it is good to minimize the use of bread, even as a part of our cooked foods.

Although bread is called the "staff of life," it is important to remember that even when the very best organic whole grains are ground at home, and organic ingredients are used, baking the bread in a 350-degree oven destroys all of the enzymes (life force), as well as a high percentage of the nutrients. Therefore, breads are included for variety and put into the "cooked foods" category. Breads should be counted in the 15% cooked portion of the evening meals.

For those desiring to bake their own bread flour, Hallelujah Acres® does carry a very fine electric grain mill, but does not do much promoting of it, because bread, no matter how good the ingredients, can only be used as a portion of the 15% cooked part of our daily food intake. This 15% portion is more for taste satisfaction, than for nutritional value.

Included in this book is a large variety of whole-grain breads to allow you to make choices and to provide variety in the 15% or cooked portion of your diet. Bon Appetite!

More About Grains

Whole grains (oats, brown rice, barley, millet, quinoa, rye, spelt, cornmeal, and buckwheat) are included in the Hallelujah Diet® because they assist the body in building muscles, increase energy, and awaken the body's metabolism. Whole grains are a source of fuel for the nervous system, muscles, hormones, brain, glands, and other organs. They are rich in many vitamins and minerals.

If you've ever heard Reverend Malkmus' *How to Eliminate Sickness* Seminar, you've heard him talk about how most commercial breads are made today. He shares how the wheat kernels are stripped of their natural ingredients and then bleached to lighten their color. After extensive processing, all that remains is a fine white powder with almost no nutrition left that the body can utilize. Due to all of the processing, these "white" flour products are so devoid of nutrition that artificial, often man-made chemicals are added back into the product so that the word "enriched" can be used on the label. Perhaps it would be profitable to look at grain kernels to see just how God created grain and why it is important to eat whole grains.

When God created grain kernels, He made them up of three parts:

1. The Bran or the "coat" (outside layer) makes up 14½% of the kernel of grain. The bran is a great source of fiber, B vitamins, phosphorus, and potassium in the diet. However, the bran is removed in the milling process and you can purchase it in your local health food store.

2. The Endosperm, which represents 83% of the cereal grain, is primarily starch that digests slowly, producing glucose or sugar that the body turns into energy. The endosperm is the source of white flour after it has been stripped of many nutrients during the milling process.

3. The Germ is the sprouting section of the grain and makes up only 2½% of each kernel of grain. It is a high source of fat and provides protein and polyunsaturated fatty acids (the good fats). You often hear that Wheat Germ is something that is supposed to be good for you and you can buy in your local health food store.

Many grains (especially wheat) contain gluten, which is an elastic protein substance that gives cohesiveness to dough. This sticky, tough protein has a tendency to form mucus in the body that may coat the villi (the tiny hair-like fibers) in the intestines. When that happens, the nutrition vitally needed by the body is hindered from proper absorption. Dr. John McDougal says on page 195 of his book, *The McDougal Plan*, "Wheat is the most common plant food to cause food allergy, and, like barley and rye, it contains a large amount of gluten. Gluten causes intestinal and other problems for some people."

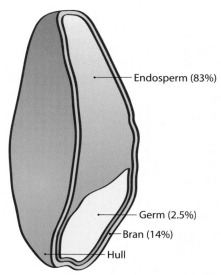

For more information on the description of grains and their uses, see *Recipes for Life ... from God's Garden.*

Note: Most bread recipes have a 1-star (★) rating because they contain unbleached white flour or other processed flour. I have noted that grains may be ground at home and oat flour may be substituted for unbleached white flour. If this is done, the star rating would improve.

LIVING FRUIT BREAD

★★★★★	Yield 36 2-inch squares
1 cup	dates, chopped
1 cup	figs, chopped
1 cup	pecans or walnuts, chopped
2 cups	ripe bananas, mashed
4 cups	raw almond butter

Combine all ingredients and knead well. Roll dough to ¼ inch and score into 2-inch squares. Place on solid Teflex sheet and dehydrate at 105 degrees for four hours. Remove from solid sheet, turn over and place on mesh sheet and dry for an additional four hours or until bread reaches desired texture.

RAW CRANBERRY BREAD
Top Raw Men

★	
2 cups	walnuts, coarsely chopped
1 cup	whole-wheat flour, freshly ground
1 cup	raw cranberries
1	apple, cored and chopped
1	orange, peeled and seeded
1 tbsp.	cinnamon
4 tbsp.	raw unfiltered honey

Process nuts and mix with whole wheat flour, set aside.

Place the cranberries, apple, and orange in a food processor using the "S" blade and process until finely ground. Add cinnamon and honey and process until mixed well. Fold into first mixture.

Spread ¼-inch thick on Teflex sheet and score into 2-inch squares. Dehydrate 4 hours at 100 degrees. Remove from sheet, turn over onto mesh dryer tray, and dry for another 4 hours.

RAW LEMON BREAD

★★★★	Yield: 16 slices
1 cup	rolled oats
2 cups	whole-grain flour
½ cup	raw unfiltered honey
1 cup	lemon juice
½ cup	strained almond milk

Use "S" blade in a food processor to break down oats to a finer consistency. Pour into large bowl and add flour, mix well. Combine honey, lemon juice, and almond milk in a separate bowl and stir to combine. Add to flour and mix and knead until the mixture becomes fine dough. Roll dough into a 3" x 8" roll, wrap in wax paper and refrigerate until firm. Slice and serve when firm.

SARDNIAN FLATBREAD
Joan Getz

★	
1 cup + 3 tsp.	distilled water
3¼ cups	semolina flour
1¼ tsp.	Celtic Sea Salt®
1½ tsp.	active dry yeast

Place in bread machine on dough cycle. When completed, divide dough into 12 pieces and roll into balls. Using a rolling pin, roll into flat circles. Let rise 20 minutes. Either bake in a 375-degree oven until lightly brown or cook on a slightly oiled griddle (extra virgin cold pressed olive oil) until slightly browned.

RAW BREAD STICKS
Top Raw Men

★★★★★	
1 cup	barley, soaked overnight in 4 cups distilled water and drained
1 cup	flaxseed
1 cup	carrot pulp
1 tbsp.	garlic powder
2 tbsp.	extra virgin cold pressed olive oil
1 tsp.	Celtic Sea Salt® (optional)
¾ cup	distilled water

Place ingredients in food processor using the "S" blade, start machine and mix well. Allow mixture to rest for thirty minutes. Roll dough into stick shape about 4 inches by one inch. Place on solid Teflex sheet and dehydrate for 6 hours. Remove from Teflex sheet; turn over onto mesh dehydrator tray and dehydrate for another 6 hours.

Variation: Sprinkle with sesame seeds before dehydrating.

TOP HAT TIP: For an easy way to transfer items from Teflex sheets to mesh grid trays, place a clean mesh grid and tray over the items on the Teflex sheet. Holding both trays securely, invert them. Carefully peel the Teflex sheet away from items, using a spatula if necessary.

BASIC ALMOND BREAD
Yvetta Myers

★★★★★	
6 cups	almonds
1 cup	ground flaxseeds (not soaked)
1 cup	extra virgin cold pressed olive oil
1 tsp.	Celtic Sea Salt® (optional)

Place almonds in food processor with "S" blade and process until they are finely ground. Add remaining ingredients and mix well. Place on solid Teflex sheets and dehydrate at 105-degrees for 6–8 hours. Transfer to mesh sheets with moist side up and dehydrate 4–8 hours.

RAW ITALIAN BREAD STICKS

★★★★★

2 cups	winter wheat berries (or any whole grain) soaked 8–12 hours, rinsed and sprouted 12–24 hours
¼ cup	fresh basil, finely chopped
½ cup	fresh parsley, finely chopped
2 cloves	garlic, peeled and minced
¼ cup	dehydrated tomato flakes*
2 tsp.	dehydrated onion flakes
3 tsp.	Vegetable Broth powder (sold in Health Food Stores)
1 tsp.	Celtic Sea Salt®
1 tsp.	Italian Seasoning
1 tsp.	date sugar (optional)

Soak winter wheat in a sprouting jar for 8–12 hours. Drain and rinse twice a day until a small tail appears. Rinse again and place in a medium size bowl.

Combine with other ingredients in a mixing bowl and set aside. Place the "S" blade in a food processor and place ½ of the ingredients in the processor bowl. Process until you have dough like consistency. Remove from food processor and place in glass bowl, process other ½ of the ingredients. Place them in the bowl with the first ½ and cover allowing to rest for 30 minutes.

Roll dough into stick shapes about 4 inches by 1 inch. Place on solid Teflex sheet and dehydrate for 6 hours. Remove from Teflex sheet; turn over onto mesh dehydrator tray and dehydrated for another 6 hours.

*Note: Dehydrated tomato flakes are made by placing ripe tomatoes in Vita Mix or blender and running machine until pureed. Pour liquid on **solid** dehydrator trays which have been coated with liquid lecithen and dehydrate at 105-degrees until leather is formed. Remove from sheet and place in Vita Mix or blender and process to flakes. Store in air tight container.

MULTI-GRAIN SUNFLOWER BREAD
Lisa Wagner

★	
1 cup	distilled water
1 cup	unbleached all-purpose flour
1 cup	whole-wheat flour
2 tbsp.	extra virgin cold pressed olive oil
2 tbsp.	raw unfiltered honey
½ cup	sunflower seeds
½ cup	rolled oats
3 tbsp.	sesame seeds
1¼ tsp.	Celtic Sea Salt®
2¼ tsp.	active dry yeast

Choose the shortest, most basic setting on your machine. This hearty bread goes great with anything. Makes a 1½ pound loaf.

"BEST" WHOLE-GRAIN BREAD
Amy McCarty

★	
1⅔ cups	distilled water
2 tsp.	Celtic Sea Salt®
1 tbsp.	molasses
1 cup	bread flour
1 cup	whole-grain flour
1 cup	rye flour
1 cup	Kamut flour
½ cup	vital gluten (may omit for dietary reasons, but will not rise as well)
3 tbsp.	non-dairy powdered milk
1–2 tbsp.	extra virgin cold pressed olive oil (optional)
3 tsp.	active dry yeast

Place in bread pan in order given. Select whole-wheat/light crust setting. Makes 2-pound loaf.

SEED BREAD
Linda Mullen

★	
1¼ cups	distilled water
¼ cup	molasses or raw unfiltered honey
⅛ tsp.	vitamin C crystals (optional–aids in rising)
2½ cups	whole-wheat flour
½ cup	unbleached all-purpose flour
2 tbsp.	vital gluten (may omit for dietary reasons, but will not rise as well)
2 tsp.	bread machine yeast
3 tbsp.	sunflower seeds
3 tbsp.	sesame seeds
2 tbsp.	flaxseeds

Place ingredients in the bread pan in the order given and bake on whole-wheat cycle.

MULTIGRAIN BREAD
Sherry Wenzel

★	Yield: one large 1½ pound loaf
1¼ cups	distilled water
2 tbsp.	butter, softened
1⅓ cups	unbleached all-purpose flour
1⅓ cups	whole-wheat flour
1 cup	8-grain cereal
3 tbsp.	raw unfiltered honey
1¼ tsp.	Celtic Sea Salt®
3 tsp.	regular active dry yeast (or 2½ tsp. bread machine yeast or 2½ tsp. quick acting yeast)

Place all ingredients in bread machine pan in order listed. Select bread type: Whole-wheat.

PEASANT BREAD
Chef Bill Paul

★	
½ cup	onions, finely chopped
3 tbsp.	butter (ghee)
1 cup + 2 tbsp.	warm rice milk
1 tbsp.	sweetener (raw unfiltered honey, date sugar, stevia, sucanat, etc.)
1 tsp.	Celtic Sea Salt®
½ tsp.	dill weed (½ tsp. basil)
½ tsp.	rosemary
¼ ounce	dry active yeast
3–3½ cups	unbleached white flour*

Sauté onions in butter. Place all ingredients in a mixing bowl except ½ cup flour, which will be used for kneading board. Knead for about 6 to 8 minutes until you have an elastic ball. Cover and let rise until doubled. Punch down. Form a ball and let rise again. Bake at 375 degrees for 25 to 30 minutes. Cool on wire rack.

*May use a mixture of unbleached all-purpose flour, whole-wheat pastry flour and/or whole-grain flour. However, the bread will probably not rise as high nor be as light in texture.

CONFETTI BREAD
Tom Brandow

★	Yields: one 1½ pound loaf:

This recipe is not only a fun recipe, but a healthy one as well. You just may sneak some veggies into your children's diet yet!

¾ cup	distilled water*
½ cup	carrot, shredded
⅓ cup	zucchini, shredded
¼ cup	green onion, diced
¼ cup	red sweet pepper, seeded and finely chopped
1 tbsp.	unsalted butter
3 cups	unbleached bread flour
1 tsp.	date sugar
¾ tsp.	Celtic Sea Salt®
½ tsp.	dried thyme, crushed, or 1½ tsp. snipped fresh thyme
1 tsp.	active dry yeast

Add the ingredients according to your bread machine directions. Run on basic white cycle.

*Note: The dough may appear stiff until the vegetables have released some of their liquid during kneading cycle. Watch closely; it may be necessary to add another 1 to 3 tbsp. of additional bread flour after the kneading cycle.

For a 2 pound loaf:	
1 cup	distilled water
⅔ cup	carrot, shredded
½ cup	zucchini, shredded
⅓ cup	green onion, diced
⅓ cup	red sweet pepper, seeded and finely chopped
4 tsp.	unsalted butter
4 cups	bread flour
1 ½ tsp.	date sugar
1 tsp.	Celtic Sea Salt®

¾ tsp.	dried thyme, crushed, or 2 tsp. snipped fresh thyme
1¼ tsp.	active dry yeast

Directions: Same as for a 1½ pound loaf.

HERB BREAD
Pat Walter

★	
½ cup	onion, chopped
3 tbsp.	extra virgin cold pressed olive oil
1½ tsp.	active dry yeast
1 cup	distilled water
3 cups	organic bread flour
1 tsp.	Celtic Sea Salt®
1½ tbsp.	raw unfiltered honey
½ tsp.	dried organic basil (crushed)
½ tsp.	organic dill weed (crushed)
½ tsp.	organic rosemary (crushed)

Sauté onion* in oil on very low heat for 10 minutes, but don't brown, just until soft. Cool for 10 minutes before adding to other ingredients in bread machine pan. Select basic white bread cycle.

*Note: While onions are cooking, put everything else in bread machine pan starting with the yeast.

ESSENE BREAD

★★★★★

The Essene's, a religious group originally based in the Dead Sea region of Israel. They were a brotherhood of Jews in Palestine from the 2nd century B. C. to the 2nd century A. D. Historically the Essene's were known for their raw vegetarian dietary philosophy, well-developed wisdom, and remarkable longevity.

¼ cup	almonds, soaked overnight and drained
¼ cup	walnuts, soaked overnight and drained
3	dates, pitted, soaked in a separate bowl until soft (about one hour) and drained
2 cups	wheat berries, kamut, or spelt*, sprouted
½	apple, peeled and shredded
1 clove	garlic, minced (optional)
1 tsp.	fresh parsley, minced
2 tbsp.	extra virgin cold pressed olive oil

Place drained sprouts and dates into food processor along with remaining ingredients and process until a dough consistency is reached. Or remove the screen and replace it with the blank on the Champion, Green Power or Green Life Juicer and run through into a catch container. Place dough on a solid dehydrating sheet and shape a loaf about 3 1/2 inches wide, about 6 inches long and 1 1/2 inches thick. Dehydrate at 100 degrees for 13 to 17 hours. The bread will be crispy on the outside and moist on the inside.

Rhonda's Kitchen Tips: Grains can be sprouted by either covering a mason jar with a piece of old nylon stocking, held in place with a rubber band, or by using a sprouting jar purchased at a health food store. Place grains in jar, cover with water, and soak seed overnight or about 12 hours. Then drain, rinse and drain again, and place in a location out of the sunlight to sprout. Then both morning and evening, rinse and drain, until little tails start to appear on the grain. Once the tails appear, the sprouts are ready to be used.

PUMPKIN CORN BREAD
Jan Jenson

★	
¾ cup	date sugar (or ½ cup raw unfiltered honey)
⅔ cup	cornmeal
¼ cup	organic butter
⅔ cup	wheat germ
	Egg Replacer to equal 2 large eggs
⅔ cup	whole-wheat flour
¾ cup	cooked, mashed pumpkin
3 tsp.	Rumford® Baking Powder*
½ cup	non-dairy milk

Mix butter and date sugar until creamy. Add Egg Replacer and beat again. Add pumpkin, milk, and cornmeal; beat till smooth. Mix flour, wheat germ, and Rumford® Baking Powder together dry; then stir into pumpkin mixture. (If you use self-rising flour or cornmeal, add it last or mixture will rise too fast and drive you nuts!) Quickly pour into 8"x8"x2" lecithin** lined pan. Bake 20-25 minutes in a 425-degree oven.

Rhonda's Kitchen Tips: Rumford® Baking Powder contains no aluminum, which can be potentially harmful to the body. It is available at health food stores and some grocery stores.

****Rhonda's Kitchen Tips:*** Liquid lecithin is a fairly thick pure vegetable product that forms a colloidal solution in water, and has emulsifying, wetting, and antioxidant properties. Place it on a paper towel and "grease" the baking dish, bread pan, or muffin tin, etc. Liquid lecithin is available in health food stores.

FLAX BANANA BREAD
Patricia Lee

★	
½ cup	sucanat, or other sweetener
½ cup	rice milk
¼ cup	fat-free egg substitute
3 tbsp.	safflower oil
¾ cup	spelt flour
½ cup	whole-grain flour
¾ cup	ground flaxseed*
1 tsp.	baking powder
1 tsp.	baking soda
⅛ tsp.	Celtic Sea Salt® (optional)
1 cup	bananas**, pureed
1 cup	nuts, chopped (optional)
½ cup	organic raisins (optional)

Preheat the oven to 350° F. Coat a no-stick 8 X 4-inch loaf pan with no-stick spray or liquid lecithin***. In a large bowl, combine the sweetener, rice milk, egg substitute, and oil. Whisk until smooth, set aside. In a medium bowl, combine the spelt flour, whole-grain flour, flaxseed, baking powder, baking soda, and salt. Whisk to mix. Add to the liquid ingredients. Stir just until blended; do not over mix. Add the prepared bananas and stir to mix.

Pour into the prepared pan. Bake for 40 to 50 minutes, or until a knife inserted in the center comes out clean. (Can use glass loaf pan and cut baking time to 25–30 minutes). Remove the pan to a wire rack and let the bread cool slightly. While it is still slightly warm, turn the bread out of the pan.

***Rhonda's Kitchen Tips:** Keep flaxseeds in refrigerator or freezer and then grind as needed. Flaxseeds can be ground in a coffee grinder, a Vita-Mix, or a blender. Ground flaxseeds may be sprinkled in shakes, over cereal, in burgers, or just make loaves and loaves of this to keep in the freezer.

**Note: For best results, choose very ripe bananas, place them in a blender or food processor, and puree until smooth.

***__Rhonda's Kitchen Tips:__ Liquid lecithin is a fairly thick pure vegetable product that forms a colloidal solution in water, and has emulsifying, wetting, and antioxidant properties. Place it on a paper towel and "grease" the baking dish, bread pan, or muffin tin, etc. Liquid lecithin is available in health food stores.

ITALIAN STYLE BREADSTICKS
Tracy Alford

★	
¾ cup	warm distilled water
2 tbsp.	extra virgin cold pressed olive oil
⅛ tsp.	Celtic Sea Salt®
1¾ cup	bread flour
1½ tsp.	active dry yeast
1 tbsp.	extra virgin cold pressed olive oil (to brush on during last few minutes of baking)

Add water, oil, sea salt, flour and yeast (in that order) to a bread machine. Run dough cycle. Remove dough from machine and place it on a lightly floured breadboard. Cut dough into 2 inch pieces. Roll, by hand, into long breadsticks. Place on cookie sheet. Let rise for 25 minutes. Pre-heat oven to 325 degrees. Bake 15 minutes, brush on olive oil and bake 5 to 10 minutes more (or until lightly browned).

Option: For additional flavor, try adding any of the following to the dough: dried Italian herbs, minced garlic, parsley, red pepper or cinnamon.

OAT BRAN MUFFINS

★	Yield: 12 large muffins

Preheat oven to 350° F.

In a medium bowl, mix together:

2 cups	Better Than Milk® or other non-dairy milk
1½ cups	oat flour with bran or wheat bran
2 cups	organic raisins, currants or chopped dates
½ cup	light or dark molasses (not Blackstrap)
½ tsp.	Celtic Sea Salt® (optional)
¼ cup	date sugar or sucanat (optional)
1–3	mashed ripe banana(s)
½ cup	chopped pecans or walnuts
½ cup	flaxseeds, ground

In a larger bowl, mix:

2 cups	flour (oat flour with bran, whole-wheat pastry or other whole-grain flour)
1 tsp.	baking soda
3 tsp.	Rumford® Baking Powder*
2 tsp.	cinnamon (optional)

Pour the milk and bran mixture into the flour mixture, and combine until moistened. Use ⅓ cup measuring cup to measure batter evenly into 12 large non-stick or liquid lecithin** lined muffin cups***. Bake for 45–50 minutes or until toothpick comes out clean. Cool on a rack.

*__Rhonda's Kitchen Tips:__ Rumford® Baking Powder contains no aluminum, which can be potentially harmful to the body. It is available at health food stores and some grocery stores.

**__Rhonda's Kitchen Tips:__ Liquid lecithin is a fairly thick pure vegetable product that forms a colloidal solution in water, and has emulsifying, wetting, and antioxidant properties. Place it on a paper towel and "grease" the baking dish, bread pan, or muffin tin, etc. Liquid lecithin is available in health food stores.

***Note: Paper muffin cups stick to very low-fat mixtures, so it is better not to use them.

This batter will keep in a covered jar or plastic container for about a week; stir batter gently before using.

Note: Muffins will keep 3–4 days, or may be frozen for future use. Also, these muffins are heavy and very filling and can be used as part of a child's breakfast.

Variations

Blueberry Muffins: Replace 2 cups Better Than Milk® or other non-dairy milk with organic unsweetened apple juice. Replace 1 cup raisins with 2 cups fresh or frozen blueberries.

Apple Muffins: Replace 2 cups Better Than Milk® or other non-dairy milk with organic unsweetened apple juice. Add 1¼ tsp. coriander and ¼ tsp. anise to dry ingredients. Replace 1 cup raisins and 1 mashed banana with 2 cups freshly peeled and shredded apples (press juice out of apples after shredding.)

Carob Muffins: Replace ½ cup flour (oat flour with bran, whole-wheat pastry or other whole-grain flour) with ½ cup carob powder. Use 1 cup chopped dates (rather than other options), 1 tsp. coffee substitute like Roma and increase to ¾ cup chopped walnuts.

Poppy Seed Muffins: Add ½ cup poppy seeds and 1 tbsp. grated lemon rind to dry ingredients.

TOASTY BREAD
Chris Palser

★

This recipe has a slightly toasty flavor and is always moist!

Place in the machine as follows:

1¼ cups	warm water
2 tbsp.	raw unfiltered honey
2 tbsp.	extra virgin cold pressed olive oil
1½ cups	unbleached white flour (golden)
1½ cups	whole-wheat flour (or other whole-grain flour)
½–¾ cup	raw sesame seeds
½–1 tsp.	Celtic Sea Salt®
2–3 tbsp.	dough enhancer
3 tsp.	yeast

Run on regular cycle, light crust.

Dough Enhancer:

In tightly sealed container combine:

1 tbsp.	ginger
1 tbsp.	vitamin C powder

COLONIAL BREAD

★	
1	package yeast
¾ cup	rye flour
¾ cup	yellow corn meal
3 cups	unbleached bread flour
1 tsp.	Celtic Sea Salt®
½ cup	raw unfiltered honey
1½ cups	very warm distilled water

Place all ingredients into pan of bread machine in the order listed, select white bread and push start.

Choose the shortest, most basic setting on your machine. Makes a 1½ pound loaf. This hearty bread goes great with anything.

Note: This is the bread we serve at the Hallelujah Acres® Restaurant in Rogersville, TN.

WHOLE-WHEAT BREAD
Joan Gertz

★	
1¼ cups	very hot distilled water
¼ cup	non-dairy milk (or omit and use 1½ cups distilled water)
4½ cups	freshly ground whole-wheat flour (or ½ whole-wheat or red wheat and ½ Prairie Gold)
3 tbsp.	extra virgin cold pressed olive oil
3 tbsp.	raw unfiltered honey
1¾ tsp.	active dry yeast
1½ tsp.	gluten flour (may omit for dietary reasons, but will not rise as well)

Place all ingredients in bread machine basket. Set machine for whole-wheat cycle. This recipe makes a light, delicious, nutritious 2-pound loaf of bread.

WHOLE-WHEAT BREAD
Becca Brasfield

★	
1½ cups	very warm distilled water (105–115 degrees)
1½ cups	unbleached all-purpose flour
1 tbsp.	extra virgin cold pressed olive oil
3 tbsp.	vital gluten (may omit for dietary reasons, but will not rise as well)
3 tbsp.	raw unfiltered honey
2 tsp.	active dry yeast
½ tsp.	Celtic Sea Salt®
⅔ cup	nine grain seed mix (from King Arthur Flour Company)
¾ cup	whole-wheat flour

Use the normal, whole-wheat cycle for a 2-pound loaf and crust color medium. Add the dough ingredients in the order listed. Add the seeds at the beep (after 50 minutes). Takes 4 hours and 20 minutes total. Cool on a rack.

Option: For smaller loaves, use the "Dough Only" cycle of the bread machine. Add the dough ingredients in the order listed. Add the seeds at the beep. This will mix, knead and do the 1st rise. (May be done by hand).

Turn out onto a floured surface and knead in flour as needed to handle the dough. Divide into two halves. Shape and place in greased loaf pans. Cover and let rise another 30–40 minutes or until doubled in size.

Bake in a pre-heated 425-degree oven for about 9 minutes in the middle of the oven. Reduce heat to 375 degrees and bake for 13–15 minutes more. Cool on racks at least 20 minutes before removing from pans. Store in refrigerator or freezer.

WHOLE-WHEAT HONEY BREAD
Gail Evans

★	
1⅛ cups	distilled water
3 cups	whole-wheat flour
1½ tsp.	Celtic Sea Salt®
⅓ cup	raw unfiltered honey
1 tbsp.	non-dairy milk powder
1½ tbsp.	extra virgin cold pressed olive oil
1½ tsp.	active dry yeast

Place wet ingredients in bread pan and then add dry ingredients and the yeast. Select whole-wheat setting and press start. Makes 1½ pound loaf.

OATMEAL BREAD
Linda Mullen

★	
1½ cups	distilled water
¼ cup	molasses or raw unfiltered honey
⅛ tsp.	vitamin C crystals (optional–aids in rising)
2½ cups	whole-wheat flour
1 cup	unbleached all-purpose flour
½ cup	quick oats
2 tbsp.	vital gluten (may omit for dietary reasons, but will not rise as well)
1 tsp.	bread machine yeast

Place ingredients in machine in order given and bake on whole-wheat cycle.

Option: Poppy-seed Onion Bread: add 2 tbsp. dried onions and 1 tbsp. poppy seeds after the yeast

Option: Cinnamon Raisin Bread: add 2 tsp. cinnamon after the yeast and about 1 cup of organic raisins at the "add ingredients" beep.

OUR DAILY BREAD
Jane Fortner

★	
3 cups	whole-wheat bread flour
1 cup + 2 tbsp.	distilled water
1 tbsp.	raw unfiltered honey
3 tsp.	quick rise yeast (Red Star gives the best results)
2 tsp.	extra virgin cold pressed olive oil

Use a setting on your machine that will approximate these times:

Knead 20 minutes, rise 30 minutes, punch down, rise 30 minutes, and bake 35 minutes at 350 degrees.

If your machine doesn't have a setting that will accommodate this recipe, use the dough setting. Take the dough out after the first rise, punch it, shape it and put it in a loaf pan in a warm oven for the second rise. At the end of the second rise, turn the oven to 350 and bake for 35 minutes. Preheating is not necessary.

WHOLE-WHEAT BREAD
Steve & Connie LaSee

★	
9½ ounces	distilled water
1 tbsp.	molasses (not Blackstrap)
1 tbsp.	raw unfiltered honey
2¼ cups	whole-wheat flour*
1 cup	bread flour
2 tbsp.	butter
2 tsp.	Active Dry Yeast

This is the only bread machine recipe I use that we all just love! I also use the recipe and put it on the dough cycle to take out and make my own buns, of which I receive lots of compliments.

Makes 1 ½-pound loaf or about 12 medium sized buns

*Note: When stone ground flour is used, add 3 tsp. wheat gluten to ensure the bread will rise as well.

WHOLE-WHEAT BREAD

Larry and Carolyn Green

★	
4½ cups	whole-wheat flour
1 tbsp.	gluten (may omit for dietary reasons, but will not rise as well)
2 tbsp.	rice "Better Than Milk" (or other non-dairy milk)
13 ounces	distilled water
2 tbsp.	Safflower oil
2 tbsp.	raw unfiltered honey
1 tbsp.	molasses (not Blackstrap)
2 tsp.	yeast

Put all wet ingredients together. Pour wet ingredients into bread machine. Put dry ingredients on top of wet and put yeast in center as usual. Bake on wheat. We have yet to find anyone who does not like this bread. Makes 2-pound loaf.

Option: We put the machine on dough (1 hour & 40 minutes). We then take out the dough, cut into two pieces. We roll out large bubbles; roll up and put into sprayed pans. We let it rise in the dehydrator for one hour. Then we bake in a convection oven until done. The results are better than baking all the way in the machine.

HONEY WHOLE-WHEAT BREAD

Myrna Bradbury

★	
4 cups	distilled water
2 tbsp.	active dry yeast
1⅓ cups	raw unfiltered honey
	whole-wheat flour as needed

This recipe does not need to rise in the pan. Knead only 3–5 minutes. Does better if the dough is left a little on the sticky side. Form into loaves. Bake at 350 degrees until done.

GRANDMA'S BREAD

★	
1½ cups	boiling distilled water
⅓ cup	yellow cornmeal
⅓ cup	molasses (not Blackstrap)
1 tsp.	Celtic Sea Salt®
1 tbsp.	butter
3½ cups	bread flour
1 pkg.	active dry yeast

Make cornmeal mush by placing cornmeal in a bowl. Carefully pour boiling water (while stirring to prevent lumps) into cornmeal, until smooth. Set aside to cool 30 minutes. When cooled, fold in molasses, salt and butter. Place yeast in bottom of bread pan then flour and top with cornmeal mush. Select white bread setting.

Options: Add dried fruit or chopped nuts.

100% WHOLE-WHEAT BREAD
Sheryl Virgil

★	
1⅓ cups	warm distilled water
2 tbsp.	extra virgin cold pressed olive oil
2 tbsp.	raw unfiltered honey or pure maple syrup
1 tsp.	Celtic Sea Salt®
2 tbsp.	vital wheat gluten (may omit for dietary reasons, but will not rise as well)
2 tsp.	Dough Enhancer (See page 184.)
3½ cups	whole-wheat flour
1 tsp.	yeast

Adjust the order of ingredients as recommended by the manufacturer of your bread machine.

WHEAT-N-HONEY BREAD
Karen Risk

★

This is a great bread-machine recipe. Place ingredients in your bread machine, in the following order:

1 tbsp.	extra virgin cold pressed olive oil
2 tbsp.	raw unfiltered honey
1⅓ cups	distilled water or non-dairy milk
1 tsp.	Celtic Sea Salt®
2 cups	bread flour
1 cup	whole-wheat flour
⅔ cup	cracked wheat
⅓ cup	wheat germ
1 heaping tsp.	wheat gluten (may omit gluten for dietary reasons, but will not rise as well)
2 scant tsp.	active dry yeast (not rapid rise yeast)

Use a basic bread setting, and light crust setting.

HONEY 7-GRAIN BREAD
Debra L. Lakes

★	
12 ounces	distilled water
¾ tsp.	Celtic Sea Salt®
1 tbsp.	grape seed oil
¼ cup	raw unfiltered honey
¾ cup	whole-wheat flour
1½ cups	7 Grain flour
¾ cup	unbleached white flour
1½ tsp.	Active Dry Yeast

All ingredients should be at room temperature (70–80 degrees F.).

This makes a 1½ pound loaf*. Best if organic ingredients are used. Put ingredients in the machine in the order listed.

Option: Add sesame seeds after the first 30 minutes.

*Note: This bread will only store for a day or two at the most; place in a plastic bag with a stalk of celery. Do not refrigerate. The remainder can be sliced and vacuum-sealed on day two. If you have a Food Saver Vacuum Sealer, be sure to freeze the slices individually before sealing them.

EZEKIEL BREAD

★	Yield: 4 loaves
7 cups	hard red winter wheat
1 cup	hulled barley
½ cup	beans, combination of dry pinto, navy, garbanzo
¼ cup	lentils
1 cup	spelt
⅓ cup	millet
5 cups	warm distilled water
½ cup	extra virgin cold pressed olive oil
½ cup	raw unfiltered honey
3 tbsp.	yeast
2 tsp.	Celtic Sea Salt®
½ cup	gluten flour (may omit for dietary reasons, but will not rise as well)

Place grains and beans in a large bowl and soak 24 hours, drain and allow them to dry 24 hours. Grind grains and beans to a flour consistency using a grain mill. In a food processor using the dough blade combine water, oil, honey, yeast and Celtic Sea Salt®. Mix gluten with multi grain/bean flour and add slowly to liquid mixture while machine is running until dough pulls away from the sides. Knead 8 to 10 minutes. Shape into 4 round loaves and place on two well greased baking sheets. Let rise and bake at 350 degrees for 40 minutes..

Holiday Delights

"O taste and see that the Lord is good...."

—Psalm 34:8

There was one other thing I was fascinated with as a young girl—cowboys! And anything "western." This is me at age 13 doing my best Dale Evans impersonation during Christmas 1958.

You will find many raw desserts with a 5 star ★★★★★ rating in this chapter. As delightful and wonderful as they are, use constraint and please don't eat these recipes every day. Many of them are too high in protein from nuts and natural sugars found in fruits, and should be used only on special occasions like Holidays!

RAW FRUIT TARTS

★★★★★	Yield: 8-inch pie plate or 6 tarts
Crust:	
1½ cups	almonds, soaked overnight and drained
1 cup	Medjool dates, pitted and chopped
1 tbsp.	raw almond butter
½	ground vanilla bean or 1 tsp. pure vanilla
¾ tsp.	cinnamon
	A few drops of apple juice, if necessary, to create the desired consistency

Process all ingredients in food processor with "S" blade to dough consistency and press into pie pan or a 6-muffin tin. Place the muffin tin in the freezer for an hour or so to set up so tart shells can be easily removed from muffin tin.

Fruit Filling:	
1 cup	pine nuts*
½ cup	orange juice, freshly squeezed
4–5	dates, pitted
½	ground vanilla bean or ½ tsp. pure vanilla

Place all ingredients in a food processor with the "S" blade and process until creamy. Spoon into tart and top with your favorite sliced fruits (slice in circles and arrange as desired).

Rhonda's Kitchen Tips: Pine nuts (pignoli or pignolia) are the edible, soft, white seed of a number of western North American pine trees. They add versatility in the kitchen with a creamy consistency when used in sauces or dressings and a wonderful texture when used whole. Because pine nuts have a very short shelf life, they should be stored in the freezer.

RAW PUMPKIN PIE TARTS

Deborah Martin

★	
1	avocado, peeled and pitted
½ cup	raw unfiltered honey
4	dates, soaked in 1 cup of water
2 tsp.	pure vanilla
1 tsp.	cinnamon
¼ tsp.	nutmeg
½ tsp.	ginger
1 tsp.	Celtic Sea Salt®
1 cup	raw macadamia nuts, soaked for 8 hours and drained
4 cups	raw pumpkin, peeled
1 cup	organic raisins
1 tsp.	psyllium powder
½ cup	pumpkin seeds, washed, soaked for 8 hours, drained and dehydrated for 6-8 hours
1	Raw Honey Nut and Date Piecrust (see recipe on page 227.)

Prior to making pumpkin filling, form tarts by pressing crust (see recipe on p. 227) into muffin tins, freeze, and remove carefully.

Place honey, vanilla, dates with soak water, cinnamon, nutmeg, ginger, salt, and macadamias into blender and blend until smooth. Add avocado and pumpkin and blend until very smooth. Add psyllium and blend well. Let this mixture sit for 15 minutes and blend well again.

Fold in raisins.

Pour pumpkin mixture into piecrust tarts and top with pumpkin seeds. Refrigerate.

APRICOT FRUIT TARTS

★★★★★ | **Yield: 6 tarts or one 8-inch pie**

Place a small amount of liquid lecithin* on a paper towel and lightly oil bottoms and sides of a 6-cup muffin tin or pie plate and set aside.

Crust:	
1½ cups	almonds, soaked overnight and drained
1 cup	Medjool dates, pitted, soaked 2 hours and drained
1 tbsp.	raw almond butter
½	vanilla bean, ground or 1 teaspoon pure vanilla
¾ tsp.	cinnamon
	a few drops of apple juice, if necessary, to create the dough-like consistency.

Process all of the above ingredients in food processor with "S" blade to dough consistency and divide crust ingredients into 6 equal parts and roll into balls. To form tarts, press 1 crust ball into each muffin tin and shape to fit tin, freeze. When tarts are frozen, carefully remove them from muffin tin.

To make a pie, place crust in pie plate and press crust to edges.

Fruit Filling:	
½ cup	dried organic apricots, cut into small pieces
3	Medjool dates, pitted and cut into small pieces
½ cup	dried organic apples, peeled and seeds removed
¼ cup	organic raisins
¼ cup	almond butter
2 tsp.	sweetener

Cut apricots and dates in pieces and cover with distilled water and soak 30 minutes. While apricots and dates are soaking, cut apples into small pieces and place in a small mixing bowl along with raisins. Drain apricots and dates, squeezing out excess water and add to raisin and apple mixture. Fold in almond butter and sweetener and mix well to coat all fruit. Fill prepared tart shells with fruit mixture. Cover and refrigerate at least one hour. Top with a dollop of Almond Whipping Cream before serving.

To make a pie, pour prepared filling into crust cover and place in refrigerator to chill.

Almond Whipping Cream:

½ cup	almond whipping cream (see recipe on page 227.)
2 tsp.	raw unfiltered honey or Agave Nectar

In a small bowl, beat cream until stiff. Fold in two teaspoons raw unfiltered honey or Agave Nectar.

RAW FUDGE

★★★★★	
1 cup	rolled oats
¾ cup	carob powder
¼ cup	sesame seeds, ground (optional)
¼ cup	sunflower seeds, ground
½ cup	raw almond nut butter
4–6	Medjool dates, pitted, soaked 2 hours and drained
½–1 cup	walnuts or pecans, chopped

Place all ingredients in food processor with S blade, and mix well. Press into 8-inch square pan lined with lecithin* or lightly oiled. Chill, cut, and serve. Keep covered in refrigerator.

Rhonda's Kitchen Tips: Liquid lecithin is a fairly thick pure vegetable product that forms a colloidal solution in water, and has emulsifying, wetting, and antioxidant properties. Place it on a paper towel and "grease" the baking dish, bread pan, or muffin tin, etc. Liquid lecithin is available in health food stores.

SNOW BALL COOKIES

★★★★★	*Yield: Approximately 25 Snow Balls*
2 cups	almonds, pecans or walnuts, soaked overnight and drained
1½ cups	dried fruit (pineapple, apple, apricots, mango, etc.)
1–2 cups	shredded unsweetened coconut
3–4	Medjool dates, soaked 2 hours and drained

Place "S" blade in food processor and turn the machine on. Alternate adding the nuts, dried fruit, and dates, and process until well mixed. In a separate bowl, place dried coconut and coat the balls before placing them on a platter.

ALMOND BUTTER CAROB CRUNCHIES

★★★★★	Yield: Approximately 21 Crunchies
¾ cup	almond butter
½ cup	carob powder
2–3	Medjool dates, pitted, soaked 2 hours and drained
1 tbsp.	distilled water
½ cup	rolled oats or toasted wheat germ
1 cup	almonds or pecans, chopped
½ cup	unsweetened coconut

Reserve 2 tbsp. coconut. Combine remaining ingredients in food processor with S blade, and mix well. Shape mixture into bite-size balls. Roll in reserved coconut. Store in plastic container with wax paper between layers in the refrigerator.

Option: May omit coconut and use chopped nuts both in recipe and to roll crunchies to coat.

RAW SUGAR PLUMS
Denise McGhie

★★★★	
1 cup	raw almonds
¾ cup	raw pecans
¾ cup	organic raisins
¾ cup	dried apricots
¾ cup	dates, chopped
¼ cup	fresh orange juice
1 cup	Shredded, unsweetened coconut

Pulse all ingredients in a food processor or blender until you have a coarse meal. Add ¼ cup fresh orange juice and pulse until mixture sticks together. Shape into 1-inch balls and roll in shredded, unsweetened coconut. Place in mini cupcake liners.

THUMBPRINT COOKIES
Deborah Martin

★★★★★

1 cup	almonds
1 cup	hazelnuts
½ cup	flax meal
1 cup	dates, pitted
1 tbsp.	orange zest
1 tbsp.	pure vanilla

Put everything except flax meal into the food processor and mix until blended well. Remove from food processor. Make flax meal by grinding the flaxseed in a coffee grinder. In a bowl add the flax meal and stir into mixture. Make small round tbsp. balls (I use a very small ice cream scoop to do this). Flatten them onto your dehydrator screen (not Teflex). Make an indentation with your thumb, and then add the fruit filling. Dehydrate at 105 degrees or until the fruit filling is firm, 8-12 hours.

Fruit Filling:	
3 dried	Turkish apricots, soaked in ½ cup of water, 4 hours
1 cup	dates, soaked
2 tbsp.	soaking water

Puree in the blender with all the water including the soak water.

Other fillings:

Replace the apricots with any of these fruits or use what you like, mangos, peaches, cherries, raspberries, or blueberries. You can use dried or fresh fruit, just don't use the extra soaking water if you use fresh fruit.

Rhonda's Kitchen Tips: Zest is the colored part of the citrus fruit (oranges, lemons, limes, grapefruit, etc.). Use the fine side of a grater or a zesting tool that can be found in kitchen stores.

HOLIDAY RAW SWEET POTATO PIE

Kathy Dean and Kathy Smith

★	Yield: two 8-inch pies
Filling:	
3	medium sweet potatoes, peeled and cut into chunks
6	dates, pitted
⅓ cup	raw unfiltered honey
¼ cup	unsweetened coconut
¾ tsp.	nutmeg
1 tsp.	fresh lemon juice
1½ tsp.	cinnamon
2–3 ounces	walnuts, ground

Peel 3 medium sweet potatoes, cut into chunks, and run through a Champion, Green Power, Green Life, or Green Star juicer, along with the 6 pitted dates, using the blank instead of the screen. In a bowl, add to the pulped sweet potato/date mixture, the remaining filling ingredients (honey, coconut, nutmeg, lemon juice, cinnamon, walnuts) and mix well.

Crust:	
1 pound	dates, pitted
1 cup	almonds, ground

Process dates and ground almonds in food processor using the "S" blade until the mixture pulls away from the sides to form a ball. Press into pie plate with wet fingers to form a crust. Add filling and cover with topping.

Topping:	
2 ounces	walnuts, ground or chopped

Refrigerate until serving time.

APPLE-PUMPKIN PIE

★

Apple portion:

3	medium apples, peeled, cored, and coarsely chopped
1 tsp.	ground cinnamon
¼ tsp.	ground allspice
¼ tsp.	ground nutmeg
1 tbsp.	oat flour
¼ cup	organic apple juice
2 tbsp.	date sugar
1	unbaked 9-inch pie shell

Preheat over to 425 degrees. Place chopped apples, cinnamon, allspice, and nutmeg over low heat and steam for 5 minutes. Stir in flour, apple juice, and date sugar. Cook 1 minute and pour into unbaked pie shell. Set aside.

Pumpkin Portion:

1 cup	organic pumpkin
	Egg Replacer to equal 1 egg
⅓ cup	date sugar
½ tsp.	ground cinnamon
¼ tsp.	ground nutmeg
¼ tsp.	ground cloves
½ cup	non-dairy milk

In a medium bowl or food processor, combine pumpkin, Egg Replacer, date sugar, cinnamon, ground nutmeg, and cloves. Mix or process until well blended. Stir in non-dairy milk and mix well. Slowly pour pumpkin mixture over apple mixture. Bake 15 minutes at 425 degrees. Reduce heat to 350 degrees and bake 30 additional minutes or until center is set.

RAW APPLE DESSERT
Jenny Hannaford

★★★★★	
5 or 6	peeled and cut into slices apples
½	fresh pineapple, peeled and diced
½ cup	dates, pitted and chopped
1 cup	pecans, coarsely chopped
1 tsp.	cinnamon (or to taste)

Mix all ingredients together and cover and place in the refrigerator for 30 minutes allowing the flavors to blend. Mix again before serving.

RAW FRUIT CAKE

★	
1 cup	organic dates, pitted
1 cup	organic raisins
1 cup	organic prunes
1 cup	pecans
1 cup	walnuts
1 cup	shredded coconut
	Raw unfiltered honey

Run through your food processor with an "S" blade the dates, raisins, and prunes. Finely chop the pecan and walnut meats and then mix with the fruit, adding the shredded coconut. Moisten all with a small amount of honey and put in mold that has been coated with liquid lecithin*.

***Rhonda's Kitchen Tips:** Liquid lecithin is a fairly thick pure vegetable product that forms a colloidal solution in water, and has emulsifying, wetting, and antioxidant properties. Place it on a paper towel and "grease" the baking dish, bread pan, or muffin tin, etc. Liquid lecithin is available in health food stores.

RAW APPLE PIE

★★★★★

Filling:	
5–6	Gala or Golden Delicious apples, peeled and cored
1 cup	organic raisins, soaked one hour with just enough water to cover, and drained (save soaking water)
¾ cup	soft dates, pitted and soaked one hour and drained
1 tbsp.	flaxseed, ground fine*
	Juice from one medium size lemon
½ cup	organic coconut, ground to a powder
1 tsp.	cinnamon
1 tsp.	nutmeg
½ tsp.	allspice

Put ½ of the apples and the water from soaked raisins into a food processor with the "S" blade until a small coarseness is achieved; pour into bowl and set aside. Place remaining ingredients in food processor with S blade and pulse the food processor off and on to process ingredients to a slightly larger consistency. Add to the first batch of apples and mix well. Put into crust and chill.

Topping:

Ground, roasted coconut with chopped walnuts or pecans. Place whole nuts around the edge if desired.

Crust:

Use any of the raw piecrust recipes found at the end of this chapter.

Rhonda's Kitchen Tips: The ground flaxseed in this recipe helps the pie to "set up" nicely so that it can be sliced.

RAW PUMPKIN PIE

★★★★★

1½–2 cups	raw pumpkin
1 cup	almonds, soaked overnight and drained
2–4 tbsp.	fresh lemon or orange juice
2–3	Medjool dates, pitted, soaked 2 hours and drained
½ cup	unsweetened coconut
½ cup	organic raisins, soaked overnight and drained
1 tsp.	cinnamon
½ tsp.	ginger
¾ tsp.	nutmeg
½ tsp.	mace (optional)

In a blender, food processor, or Vita-Mix, combine the pumpkin, almonds, juice and soaked dates and process until creamy. If too thin, add more almonds and process until creamy (the consistency should be that of pancake batter). Pour into mixing bowl and fold in coconut, raisins, and spices. Pour into prepared piecrust, cover, and chill overnight. The pie will firm up some when chilled.

RED, WHITE, AND BLUE PARFAIT

★★★★

3	bananas, peeled and frozen
2 cups	blueberries, fresh or frozen
2 cups	raspberries or strawberries, fresh or frozen
½ cup	organic apple juice
¾ cup	nuts, chopped

Chop the nuts and place a few in the bottom of each glass. In a Vita-Mix place the bananas and apple juice and process until the bananas are creamy. Place blueberries or strawberries over the nuts, then a layer of banana ice cream, and then the other berry and continue to layer until the parfait glass is filled. Top with a few chopped nuts. Place in the freezer to set firm before serving.

BANANA DATE-NUT OATMEAL COOKIES

★★★	
3	bananas, mashed
1 cup	dates, chopped
1 cup	raisins
1 cup	unsweetened coconut
½ cup	pecans, coarsely chopped
1 tsp.	pure vanilla
½ tsp.	Celtic Sea Salt® (optional)
2 cups	rolled oats

Mash bananas; add all other ingredients, adding oats last. If leaving them raw, just roll into small balls and refrigerate. If baking, drop by tbsp. and flatten on a Teflon coated baking pan and bake at 350 degrees for 15–20 minutes. You might like to try them both ways on that first batch to see which way you like them best.

HAWAIIAN DELIGHT CAKE

★★★	
	Egg substitute equal to 2 eggs
1¼ cups	whole-wheat flour
1 cup	whole-wheat pastry flour or unbleached white flour
2 tsp.	Rumford® Baking Powder*
2½ cups	unsweetened crushed pineapple in its own juice
1 cup	dates, diced
½ cup	unsweetened shredded coconut

Combine dry ingredients and mix well. Beat egg substitute and combine with pineapple, diced dates and coconut. Mix all ingredients together and pour into a 9"x 13" pan and bake at 350 degrees for 40–45 minutes.

Rhonda's Kitchen Tips: Rumford® Baking Powder contains no aluminum, which can be potentially harmful to the body. It is available at health food stores and some grocery stores.

CARROT CAKE—RAW

(consistency of fudge)

★★★★★

½ cup	raisins, soaked twenty minutes in enough distilled water to cover them
½ cup	dried apricots, soaked as above but in it's own bowl
2 cups	pecans, walnuts, or other nuts of your choice
2 tbsp.	pine nuts*
1½ cups	raw coconut
1½ tsp.	cinnamon
1 tsp.	coriander
Pinch	ground nutmeg
Pinch	ground clove
6 cups	organic carrot pulp
1½ cups	dates, pitted and chopped

While the fruit is soaking, make carrot pulp by using the blank instead of the screen so the pulp comes out the pulp ejector on a Green Power, Green Life, or Champion.

In a food processor or Vita-Mix, combine the nuts and pine nuts, with an S blade and process until fine. Add coconut and pulse a few more times until mixed. Add the spices and pulse until mixed. Set aside.

With the blank still in place, alternate putting the carrot pulp, raisins, apricots and dates through the machine and into a bowl. Knead this mixture with wet hands until the ingredients are evenly combined. Add the nut mixture a little at a time, kneading it in.

Firmly pack the mixture into a form pan or mold. This recipe is large enough to use several small molds or put into two 8-inch layer pans. If making a layer cake, use unsweetened coconut rather than a frosting between layers.

This will keep several days if refrigerated.

Rhonda's Kitchen Tips: Pine nuts (pignoli or pignolia) are the edible, soft, white seed of a number of western North American pine trees. They add versatility in the kitchen with a creamy consistency when used in sauces or dressings and a wonderful texture when used whole. Because pine nuts have a very short shelf life, they should be stored in the freezer.

FRESH FRUIT "JELLO"

★★★

2½ cups	fresh or organic apple juice (or other fresh or organic fruit juice)
1½ tbsp.	agar agar flakes
2 pints	fresh fruit
3 tbsp.	unsweetened coconut (optional)
1 tsp.	pure vanilla extract (optional)

Clean fruit, remove stems and cut fruit into bite size pieces, if necessary. Place in a bowl and set aside.

Place agar agar flakes and ½ cup juice in a small pan and bring to a simmer. Simmer five minutes until agar agar is dissolved, stirring occasionally. Remove from heat and fold in coconut and vanilla. Cool 15 minutes before adding remaining juice and fresh fruit. Mix well. Pour into a decorative ring or mold and chill several hours or overnight.

Option: Before putting in the mold or pan, 6 ounces of a fresh fruit smoothie may be folded in, if desired. See Fruit Smoothie recipe, on page 34.

"CREAM CHEESE" FROSTING

★

8 ounces	non-dairy cream cheese
8 tbsp.	non-dairy margarine
2–4 tbsp.	raw unfiltered honey
½ cup	pecans, chopped

Beat cream cheese and margarine until light and fluffy, add honey and mix well. Fold in nuts.

HAWAIIAN BUNDT CAKE

★	
⅓ cup	extra virgin cold pressed olive oil
6	Medjool dates, pitted, soaked 2 hours and drained
½ cup	unsulphered molasses
1 cup	Rice Better Than Milk (2 tbsp. powder to 1 cup distilled water)
1 medium	apple, peeled and shredded or finely grated
2 cups	carrots, shredded or finely grated
1 8-ounce can	crushed pineapple (in its own juice; do not drain)
1 cup	dates or raisins, chopped and soaked (see instructions on following page)
½ cup	pecans, chopped
½ cup	grated coconut (optional)
2 cups	whole-wheat pastry flour
1 cup	oat flour
1 cup	unbleached all-purpose flour
1 tbsp.	Rice Better Than Milk powder
3 tsp.	Egg Replacer
2 tsp.	baking soda
1 tsp.	Rumford® Baking Power*
1 tsp.	cinnamon
½ tsp.	ginger
½ tsp.	cloves
¼ tsp.	nutmeg

Dates or Raisins: Place in small bowl and cover with boiling water. Allow to sit until needed; drain before adding to other ingredients.

In a food processor using the "S" blade, combine oil, dates, molasses, and Better Than Milk liquid. Process to mix well.

In a large bowl, place grated carrots, apple, pineapple with juice, drained dates or raisins, chopped nuts and coconut, if using. Fold in liquid ingredients from food processor.

In a separate bowl, mix flour, Better Than Milk, egg replacer, baking soda, baking powder, and spices. Add dry ingredients slowly stirring constantly or while using a mixer. Pour cake batter (it will be thick) into a bundt pan or 9" x 13" cake pan that has been sprayed with olive oil.

Bake 40–50 minutes in 350-degree oven or until a toothpick inserted in the middle comes out clean.

Glaze:	
½ cup	freshly squeezed orange juice
2 tsp.	arrowroot powder
1 tsp.	raw unfiltered honey

Combine all ingredients and mix until arrowroot is dissolved. Place in a small saucepan and heat until slightly thickened. Pour over cake.

__Rhonda's Kitchen Tips:__ Rumford® Baking Powder contains no aluminum, which can be potentially harmful to the body. It is available at health food stores and some grocery stores.

ROYAL FROSTING

★	
½ cup	non-dairy margarine
½ cup	raw unfiltered honey
½ cup	Better Than Milk Powder
1 tsp.	pure vanilla
1 tsp.	orange rind, grated fine (zest)
	Pinch of Celtic Sea Salt® (⅛ tsp. or less, optional)

Mix until creamy consistency is reached and spread on cake. May sprinkle cake with unsweetened grated coconut for added appeal.

__Rhonda's Kitchen Tips:__ Zest is the colored part of the citrus fruit (oranges, lemons, limes, grapefruit, etc.). Use the fine side of a grater or a zesting tool that can be found in kitchen stores.

BANANA CREAM PIE

★	
3 tbsp.	agar agar flakes soaked in ½ cup cold distilled water
1½ cups	almond milk (see recipe on page 35)
¼ cup	pure maple syrup
½ tsp.	Celtic Sea Salt® (optional)
1 tsp.	pure vanilla or one vanilla bean, ground
5 large	ripe (speckled) bananas, sliced

Place one banana, agar agar, and water mixture in a blender and mix well. Pour into a small saucepan and allow to set 5 minutes until agar agar softens. When softened, add almond milk, maple syrup, and sea salt and mix well. Place on medium heat stirring constantly with a wire whisk or spoon. Heat until slightly thickened. Remove from heat and quickly fold in vanilla and prepared sliced bananas. Pour into prepared crust; allow to slightly cool; cover with plastic wrap and refrigerate. Pie sets up as it cools.

Option: Add some ground dehydrated pineapple for a little added flavor.

BREAD PUDDING

Preheat oven to 350 degrees.

Place in lecithin* lined 8-inch square pan:

4 cups	dry whole-grain bread, cubed (trim crusts if desired)

Mix the following in a blender:

1¾ cups	non-dairy milk
3	Medjool dates, soaked 1 hour and drained
¼ tsp.	Celtic Sea Salt® (optional)
Add:	
½ cup	organic raisins or currants

Pour the blended mixture over the bread, sprinkle generously with cinnamon and/or nutmeg add raisins and mix well. Let stand for about 20 minutes. Set the 8-inch pan inside a larger pan with hot water in it.

Bake for 30 minutes. Serve hot or cold.

Rhonda's Kitchen Tips: Liquid lecithin is a fairly thick pure vegetable product that forms a colloidal solution in water, and has emulsifying, wetting, and antioxidant properties. Place it on a paper towel and "grease" the baking dish, bread pan, or muffin tin, etc. Liquid lecithin is available in health food stores.

FROZEN BANANA CREAM PIE

★★★★★

5–6	ripe bananas, peeled
½ cup	coconut
½ cup	dates, chopped
1 tsp.	pure vanilla or ground vanilla bean
	Fresh or frozen fruit

Place bananas, coconut, chopped dates, and vanilla in a food processor using an "S" blade or in blender and blend until a creamy consistency is reached. Pour into prepared Nutty Crust (see recipe on page 228) and top with desired fruit. Freeze overnight or until frozen solid.

Option: Omit fruit and add 1 tbsp. carob powder to banana mixture.

RASPBERRY PIE
Brenda-Joyce Garner

★★★★

Combine the following ingredients for a crust, then press and shape them to line a pie plate.

1 cup	whole-wheat flour, freshly ground (I sometimes sprout the wheat, let it dry, then grind it.)
¼ cup	raw almonds, freshly ground
½ cup	dates, ground

In a food processor with S blade, puree dates and then fold in raspberries and fill pie shell with the mixture:

4 cups	raspberries (or blackberries, or boysenberries, etc.)
6	dates, pitted, soaked for one hour and drained

Chill and serve. Or decorate with sliced bananas, fresh peach slices, other fruits of your choice, or even flowers.

RAW "APPLE PIE"
Jenny Hannaford

★★★★

This combination tastes wonderful and satisfies the urge for that "apple pie" taste. I've served it to confirmed junk-food-a-holics and they always want more.

5 or 6	apples, cut into fork-sized chunks (peel if you prefer)
½	fresh pineapple, de-skinned and diced
½–1 cup	dates, pitted and chopped
1–2 tsp.	cinnamon (depending on your taste and the size of your apples)
1 cup	pecans, shelled (whole or very coarsely chopped)

Mix and let set 30 minutes or so to let the flavors blend. Mix again before serving.

"FRUIT MELODY SURPRISE"
Thomas Villalon

★★★★

1	apple, peeled and diced
1	banana, diced
	A handful of grapes, seeded
several	strawberries, quartered
1 full scoop	raisins

Mix all of the above items and place in custard dish. Put in refrigerator for about 30 minutes to chill, serve cold. Use for a great after dinner snack. Feel free to add any other fruits in season.

HONEY PEACH FREEZE
Tami Duvall

★	
1 pound	frozen peaches
2 tbsp.	raw unfiltered honey
1½ tbsp.	Orange Juice
2 tsp.	Lemon Juice

Set aside a few peach slices for garnish if desired. Place remaining peaches in a blender or food processor; add honey and juices. Cover and process until smooth. Eat now or pour into four freezer containers. Freeze. Remove from the freezer 5 minutes before serving. Garnish with reserved peaches. Or you can pour into Popsicle molds and freeze.

Note: This recipe has a 1-star (★) rating because of the honey.

NO BAKE OATMEAL COOKIES
Greg Bennett

★	Yield: 12
⅓ cup	raw unfiltered honey
¼ cup	almond or other non-dairy milk
1 tbsp.	carob powder
1 cup	rolled oats
¼ tsp.	pure vanilla
¼ cup	chopped almonds, pecans, or walnuts
4	dates, pitted

Mix honey, milk, and carob in pan. Heat until boiling, then remove from heat source. Blend all ingredients together. Spoon batter into 1-inch balls and place on wax paper. Refrigerate. May omit the nuts if desired, and use less carob powder for a weaker "chocolate" flavor.

CAROB PEPPERMINT HEDGEHOG BALLS

Tony Bath

★	Yield: about 24

Hello from Australia! I have a really yummy recipe that is a big all-time favorite in my family (there are 9 of us all together).

1 cup	dates, pitted
1 cup	organic raisins
1 cup	raw almonds
2 cups	rolled oats
1 cup	shredded unsweetened coconut
2 tbsp.	carob powder
2 tsp.	pure vanilla essence (extract)
½ tsp.	peppermint essence (extract)
2 tbsp.	raw unfiltered honey or apple juice concentrate

Place the dates and raisins in the food processor or blender and blend into small pieces. Add the almonds, oats, coconut, and carob powder. Blend until the mixture resembles breadcrumbs. Add the essence and the apple juice concentrate/honey. Stop the machine and check if the texture is correct by taking a small amount into the palm of your hand and rolling it up firmly into a ball. If the mixture does not bind, add extra apple juice concentrate/honey.

KEY LIME PUDDING

★★★★	
1	ripe avocado, peeled and pitted
1	ripe banana, peeled
	Juice of ½ lemon and ½ lime

Place all ingredients in a blender or food processor and process until creamy.

DATE AND NUT BALLS

★★★★★	Yield: about 24
2 cups	organic dates, pitted and soaked 30 minutes
1 cup	almonds, pecans or walnuts, soaked overnight and drained
1½ cups	shredded unsweetened coconut
1 tsp.	cinnamon
½ tsp.	pure vanilla or ½ vanilla bean, ground

Place nuts in a bowl and add 2 cups of distilled water. Cover with a cloth and allow the nuts to soak overnight. After soaking, drain and set aside. Pit dates and place in a bowl; cover with distilled water and soak thirty minutes. Put "S" blade in a food processor and add soaked nuts. Pulse until the nuts are finely chopped; add 1 cup of coconut, cinnamon, and vanilla and pulse until well mixed. Add the soaked dates a few at a time, processing until well mixed. Transfer to a large bowl and knead. Roll into balls and roll balls in extra coconut or chopped nuts, if desired. These nut balls will keep about 2 weeks in the refrigerator or longer in the freezer.

NO BAKE COOKIES

★★★★★	
1 cup	almonds
1 cup	rolled oats
2 cups	organic raisins
1 tsp.	cinnamon, optional
¼ tsp.	nutmeg, optional

In a food processor with an "S" blade running, chop almonds. Mix with rolled oats and put through the machine a second time. Add raisins and put the mixture through the machine one last time.

Press into an eight (8) inch square pan. Top with grated coconut or minced nuts, if desired. Cover and refrigerate before cutting into 2- inch squares.

BANANA ROLL-UPS
Charli Ayster

★	
	Whole-grain tortillas
1 tbsp.	raw unfiltered honey
1 tbsp.	raw almond butter
Sprinkle	organic raisins
	Bananas

Cut banana into 2-inch pieces and combine with honey and almond butter. Spread on tortilla. Sprinkle with raisins and roll it up.

Option: Replace the honey with 2 soaked, pitted, and pureed dates and this becomes a 3-star (★★★) recipe.

COCONUT-PECAN FROSTING

★	
1 cup	unsweetened coconut, toasted
1 cup	pecans, chopped and toasted
2 tbsp.	arrowroot powder dissolved in 2 tbsp. distilled water
1 cup	pure maple syrup
½ cup	distilled water
½ tsp.	Celtic Sea Salt® (optional)

Dry roast coconut and chopped nuts in a pan over medium heat, stirring constantly, until coconut is lightly browned. Set aside. Mix arrowroot powder and 2 tbsp. distilled water; stir until dissolved. Set aside. In a small saucepan combine maple syrup, distilled water, Celtic Sea Salt®, and arrowroot mixture and heat until boiling, stirring constantly. As it begins to thicken, stir in coconut and chopped nuts. Cook one minute. Cool to almost room temperature before using (mixture thickens as it cools).

GERMAN CAROB CAKE

★	
1½ cups	whole-wheat pastry flour
1½ cups	unbleached white flour
1 cup	toasted carob powder
3 rounded tsp.	Rumford® Baking Powder*
½ tsp.	Celtic Sea Salt®
2 tbsp.	Egg Replacer
¼ cup	grape seed oil
12 ounces	apple juice or apple juice concentrate
½ cup	pure maple syrup
2 tbsp.	Roma (or other coffee substitute), mixed in ¾ cup distilled water
1 tsp.	pure vanilla

Mix all dry ingredients together in a bowl, mix thoroughly and make "well" in the center. In another bowl, mix all wet ingredients then pour wet ingredients into the dry "well." Beat with an electric mixer until smooth, but do NOT over mix. The consistency will be that of brownies. Pour into lecithin** lined 9"x13" pan, two round cake pans, or a bundt cake pan. Bake at 350 degrees for 35–40 minutes. Cool slightly before turning onto a rack to cool completely. Frost cake with the Coconut-Pecan Frosting, see recipe on page 219.

*__Rhonda's Kitchen Tips:__ Rumford® Baking Powder contains no aluminum, which can be potentially harmful to the body. It is available at health food stores and some grocery stores.

**__Rhonda's Kitchen Tips:__ Liquid lecithin is a fairly thick pure vegetable product that forms a colloidal solution in water, and has emulsifying, wetting, and antioxidant properties. Place it on a paper towel and "grease" the baking dish, bread pan, or muffin tin, etc. Liquid lecithin is available in health food stores.

BANANA NUT BREAD

★	Yield: 1 loaf
	Juice of 1 lemon
3	very ripe bananas, peeled
½ cup	raw unfiltered honey
¼ cup	raw applesauce
¼ cup	vegetable oil
1½ cups	whole-grain flour
½ cup	wheat germ
½ tsp.	Celtic Sea Salt®
½ tsp.	baking powder
½ tsp.	baking soda
¾–1 cup	nuts (like pecan or walnuts)
1 cup	dates, chopped (optional)

Preheat oven to 375-degrees.

Using a mixer, mash bananas and mix in lemon juice until smooth. Add honey, oil, and applesauce. In separate bowl, mix dry ingredients. Add to banana mix until combined. Stir in nuts, etc., by hand. Turn into a lecithin* lined loaf pan and bake 30–45 min. To test for doneness, insert a knife into the loaf; it's done if it comes out clean. Freezes well.

*__Rhonda's Kitchen Tips:__ Liquid lecithin is a fairly thick pure vegetable product that forms a colloidal solution in water, and has emulsifying, wetting, and antioxidant properties. Place it on a paper towel and "grease" the baking dish, bread pan, or muffin tin, etc. Liquid lecithin is available in health food stores.

PUMPKIN PIE OR PUDDING
Claudia Jacobi

★	
½ cup	raw almonds, soaked overnight and drained
¾ cup	distilled water
2½–3½ cups	pumpkin
⅓ cup	raw unfiltered honey
2 tbsp.	pure maple syrup
1½ tsp.	powdered vanilla bean (or ½ tsp. pure vanilla)
1¼ tsp.	cinnamon
¼ cup	arrowroot powder

Blend almonds and water in blender until creamy; pour into bowl. Add remaining ingredients and whip with a wire whisk to mix well. Pour into unbaked pie shell and bake at 350 degrees for one hour.

For pudding: Pour filling into saucepan, and cook until thickened, stirring constantly. Serve in parfait dishes, alternating pudding with a little Almond Whipping Cream (see recipe on page 227). Garnish with mint leaves.

YUMMY CAROB PUDDING

★★★★★	
1½ cups	dates, seeded and soaked for one hour in a small amount of organic apple juice
2	medium ripe avocados, peeled and pitted
½ cup	carob powder

Place all ingredients in Vita-Mix or blender and process until a creamy consistency is reached; stop blender, scrape sides and blend again. Place in small dessert dishes, cover, chill and serve. Will keep up to 24 hours in the refrigerator.

CARROT PULP COOKIES
Claudia Jacobi

★	Yield: approximately 100 2½-inch cookies
4 cups	carrot pulp
2 cups	oat flour
1 cup	walnuts, chopped
1 cup	pecans, chopped
2 cups	Fuji apples, pureed
1½ cups	carob chips
1½ cups	organic raisins or currants
1 cup	raw unfiltered honey
1 tbsp.	cinnamon
1½ tsp.	pure vanilla extract (I use Frontiers®)

Place all ingredients in a dishpan to give lots of room for mixing. Mix with a large spoon or with your hands. Scoop out mixture with a soupspoon from your flatware. Make cookie shape in the palm of your hand, using the back of the spoon to help with the shaping. Plop onto dehydrator tray with **solid** Teflex sheet in place, and press down on cookie to make it spread to about a 2 ½-inch cookie size. You can get 25 cookies on one tray. (Remember they don't get bigger.) Place trays every other shelf to allow for good air circulation and dehydrate at 105 degrees for 6 hours. Remove Teflex sheet, return cookies to **screened** tray and dehydrate for 1–2 more hours. Let cool. Place in a sealed container and refrigerate.

If you don't have a dehydrator, place cookies on cookie sheet and bake at 200 degrees for 3 hours. The cookies won't be a live food, but they are still really good!

CARROT CAKE–BAKED

★	
½ cup	warm distilled water
2 tbsp.	dry yeast
2 tsp.	raw unfiltered honey
1½ cups	carrots, finely grated
½ cup	nuts, chopped
1 cup	organic raisins
1½ tsp.	lemon or orange rind, grated
1 tsp.	cinnamon
½ tsp.	coriander or nutmeg
Pinch	anise (optional)
½ cup	shredded unsweetened coconut
1½ cups	unbleached white flour
¾–1 cup	whole-wheat pastry flour
½ cup	non-dairy milk
¾ cup	raw unfiltered honey
1 tsp.	pure vanilla
1 tsp.	maple flavoring
⅓ cup	applesauce* (to replace oil that would normally be used)

Combine first three ingredients in a small bowl. Set aside in a warm place to bubble for about 10 minutes. While sponge is forming, wash, grate, and measure carrots. Put into another bowl and add next six ingredients. Mix well. Blend remaining ingredients on high for one minute. Add to carrots and mix together. When sponge is ready, add to bowl and stir together quickly. Evenly spread into lecithin** lined 8″ x 8″ baking pan. Bake 375 degrees for 15 minutes. Reduce heat to 350 degrees and continue baking for 40–45 minutes more. Cake is done when toothpick inserted in the center comes out clean.

*Note: The consistency with the applesauce is not quite what it would be with the oil, but it is healthier! If you choose to use the oil, just remember that heated oil can be potentially harmful to the body so eat it sparingly!

**Rhonda's Kitchen Tips: Liquid lecithin is a fairly thick pure vegetable product that forms a colloidal solution in water, and has emulsifying, wetting, and antioxidant properties. Place it on a paper towel and "grease" the baking dish, bread pan, or muffin tin, etc. Liquid lecithin is available in health food stores.

ALMOND DATE PIECRUST

★★★★★	
2 cups	almonds, soaked overnight and drained
1 cup	dates, or organic raisins, soaked for 2 hours and drained
1 tbsp.	organic apple juice
1 tsp.	pure vanilla
Dash	cinnamon

In a food processor using an "S" blade or grinder, grind nuts until fine. In a food processor using an "S" blade, process dates or raisins until they are finely ground. Add apple juice, vanilla, and cinnamon through the chute while the machine is running. The crust should appear damp and hold together. Add more juice by the tsp. full if needed. Wet hands and press crust thinly into a pie plate (from the center to the outside rim).

VANILLA FROSTING

★	Yield: 1 ½ cups (Frosts 2 9-inch cakes or 1 Bunt cake)
1 cup	non-dairy "cream cheese"
3 tbsp.	non-dairy milk powder
2 tsp.	pure vanilla
¼–½ cup	brown rice syrup (or maple syrup)

In a chilled mixing bowl combine and mix well, "cream cheese," non-dairy milk powder, and vanilla, and brown rice syrup.

ALL-IN-ONE VEGAN CAROB CAKE

★	(Serves 8)
1 tbsp.	raw unfiltered apple cider vinegar
1 cup	non-dairy milk
1⅔ cups	whole-wheat pastry flour
⅔ cup	unsweetened carob powder
1½ cups	sweetener
1½ tsp.	baking soda
1 tsp.	Celtic Sea Salt® (optional)
2 tsp.	Ener-G Egg Replacer
¼ cup	distilled water
1 tsp.	pure vanilla
½ cup	distilled water
½ cup	soft non-dairy margarine

Preheat oven to 350 degrees. On a paper towel pour about 1 tbsp. of liquid lecithin* and "oil" 2 round layer pans, 8" x 1½", then lightly coat with flour. Set aside. Put vinegar in cup and add non-dairy milk, whisk until well mixed. Place flour, carob, sweetener, baking soda, and sea salt in large bowl and mix together well with spoon. Mix Egg Replacer and ¼ cup water until smooth. Add margarine, vanilla, soured non-dairy milk, ½ cup water, and mixed Egg Replacer to dry ingredients in bowl. Beat with electric mixer for 3 minutes at medium speed, scraping bowl frequently. Pour into prepared pans.

Bake for 30 to 35 minutes at 350 degrees, or until wooden toothpick inserted in center of cake comes out clean. Remove from oven and let cool in pans for 5 minutes. Remove from pans and cool on cake rack until cold. Frost as desired.

Rhonda's Kitchen Tips: Liquid lecithin is a fairly thick pure vegetable product that forms a colloidal solution in water, and has emulsifying, wetting, and antioxidant properties. Place it on a paper towel and "grease" the baking dish, bread pan, or muffin tin, etc. Liquid lecithin is available in health food stores.

ALMOND WHIPPING CREAM

★★★	
2 ¾ cups	distilled water
1 tbsp.	each arrowroot and oat flour
6–8	chopped dates, pitted, soaked and drained
1 cup	almonds*, soaked overnight and drained
1½ tsp.	pure vanilla
½ tsp.	Celtic Sea Salt®

Blend ¾ cup distilled water and other ingredients in a Vita-Mix or blender until creamy; pour into a bowl and set aside. Bring the remaining 2 cups of distilled water to a boil; pour blender ingredients into boiling water while stirring constantly with a wire whisk. Stir and cook until thickened nicely. Chill and serve as you would any other whipping cream.

*Note: For a "whiter" cream, pour boiling water over almonds and allow them to soak 5 minutes; drain and remove skins.

RAW HONEY NUT
AND DATE PIECRUST
Deborah Martin

★	
1 cup	pecans, soaked 12 hours, drained and dehydrated 12 hours
1 cup	walnuts, soaked 12 hours, drained and dehydrated 12 hours
½ cup	raw unfiltered honey
1 tsp.	Celtic Sea Salt®
1 cup	dates, pitted
1 tsp.	pure vanilla

Place all ingredients in a food processor and process until it begins to form a ball. Remove small amounts of piecrust. Press into pie plates or muffin tins. Continue until entire pie plate is covered. Wrap in wax paper until ready to fill. Crust may be made ahead of time and refrigerated or frozen. Crust may be used as is or dehydrated for a dryer crust. Some of the crust may be put aside to use as crumbles on top of the pie.

RAW NUTTY CRUST

★★★★★	
2 cups	nuts (walnuts, pecans, almonds, or combination), soaked overnight and drained
¾ cup	organic dates, pitted and chopped and soaked for 3 hours, drained
1 tsp.	pure vanilla or ground vanilla bean
1–3 tbsp.	fresh apple juice or distilled water

Place "S" blade in Cuisinart or other food processor; turn machine on and feed nuts and dates through the chute. Process until a fine texture is reached. With machine running, add liquid one tbsp. at a time until nuts cling together. Stop machine; remove mixture and press into a glass pie plate. Fill with desired filling. The Raw Pumpkin Pie (see *page 206 for recipe.*) works well, as does the Banana Cream Pie filling (see *page 212 for recipe.*)

BASIC PIE SHELL

★★★	
½ cup	raw nuts
½ cup	quick rolled oats
1 cup	whole-grain flour
½ cup	distilled water

Grind nuts and oats in dry blender. Put in bowl. Add whole-grain flour and mix dry ingredients well. Add water. May be rolled out between wax paper or pressed into pie plate and rolled with pizza roller. This crust is easy to flute, if desired. Bake at 350 degrees for 25 minutes.

NUT AND DATE PIECRUST

Jackie Graff, R.N., B.S.N., Raw Foods Chef

★★★★★	
1 cup	almonds, soaked 12 hours, drained, and dehydrated for 12 hours
1 cup	pecans, soaked 12 hours, drained, and dehydrated for 12 hours
1 cup	walnuts, soaked 12 hours, drained, and dehydrated for 12 hours
1½ cups	Medjool dates, pits removed
½ tsp.	Celtic Sea Salt®
1 tsp.	vanilla powder*

Place almonds in food processor and process until mixture resembles flour. Add salt and vanilla to the almonds and process well. Place pecans, walnuts, and dates in food processor and process just until mixed well. Press mixture into 8- to 10-inch pie pan. Crust may be made ahead of time and refrigerated or frozen. This recipe makes a very thick crust.

***Jackie's Kitchen Tip**: Make vanilla powder by placing whole, dried vanilla beans in food processor and grinding them to a powder. Store in airtight container and use wherever liquid extract would be used.

Gifts To Share

*"For God so loved the world that he gave his only begotten Son,
that whosoever believeth in him should not perish, but have
everlasting life."*

—John 3:16

———————————————

*George put the camera on a self-timer, and rushed over to pose for
this happy moment during Christmas of 1997. I've shared so many
wonderful holidays with so many loved ones. In this picture, I am
with my one true love.*

*T*he antique blue canning jars or other unique jars makes these gifts extra special; try adding some ribbon or a lid that is embroidered or quilted. Use your imagination and creativity to make a gift that is uniquely you! Here are a few ideas to get you started. Be creative and see if you can convert some of your favorite recipes to gift ideas.

COOKIES IN A JAR

Yield: 1 holiday gift jar or holiday tin

See pages 199–200 for Snow Ball Cookies, Almond Butter Carob Crunchies, and Raw Sugar Plum recipes. Prepare several kinds as you can mix them in your gift jars or even in a nice tin.

BARLEY AND PEA SOUP MIX

Yield: 1 quart gift jar

1 cup	red lentils
½ cup	green split peas
½ cup	yellow split peas
¾ cup	pearled barley
1 tsp.	Celtic Sea Salt®
2 tsp.	garlic powder
¼ cup	dehydrated celery flakes
¼ cup	dehydrated parsley flakes
½ tsp.	dried thyme
	Cayenne pepper to taste (optional)

Layer ingredients in the order given into a 1-quart wide-mouth canning jar. Lightly tap jar to pack each layer before adding next ingredient.

Attach the following directions: Place soup mix in a large stockpot. Add 16 cups distilled water. Bring to a boil, reduce heat to lowest heat and cover pan. Simmer until peas are tender, stirring occasionally.

MEXICAN BEAN SOUP MIX

1 pound	black beans
1 pound	red beans
1 pound	northern beans

Combine beans in a large bowl; mix well. Place 2 heaping cups of beans in a wide-mouth canning jar with a sealed packet of seasoning.

Seasoning Mix: (1 packet)

1 tbsp.	dried parsley flakes
2 tsp.	Mexican Seasoning (Frontier Herbs® has mixture)
¼ tsp.	garlic powder
½ tsp.	Celtic Sea Salt®
	Pinch of Cayenne pepper (optional)

Attach the following directions:

Serves 8–10

Soup Beans

2	onions, peeled and quartered
2 cloves	garlic, peeled and minced
1	organic bell pepper, seeded and chopped
1 cup	organic corn kernels
2 cups	organic whole, peeled tomatoes

Thoroughly wash mixed beans, cover with water and soak overnight. Drain. Place in soup pot and add vegetables, seasoning packet, and enough distilled water to cover. Simmer 3 to 4 hours. Stir occasionally, adding more distilled water as needed.

HOT CAROB WHIP

See page 29 for recipe. Increase ingredients to fill the size jar you are using. Be sure to attach the directions!

MINESTRONE SOUP MIX

Yield: 1 gift jar	
1 cup	organic dried kidney beans
½ cup	organic black beans
½ cup	organic garbanzo beans
8	crumbled vegetable bouillon cubes
1 tsp.	dried oregano
1 tsp.	dried basil
¼ tsp.	dried thyme
2 tsp.	dried parsley
1 tsp.	Celtic Sea Salt®
Dash	cayenne pepper
2 cups	whole-grain pasta

Layer the first four ingredients in the order given into a 1-quart wide-mouth canning jar. Lightly tap jar to pack each layer before adding the next. Combine the seasonings, mix well, and place them in a small plastic bag or plastic wrap on top of the mixture. Wrap pasta in plastic and put on top.

Attach the following directions:	
Serves 4–6	
1 jar	Minestrone Soup Mix
1 cup	carrots, diced or shredded
4	celery ribs (stalks), diced
1 cup	onion, chopped
1 clove	garlic, minced
1 cup	cabbage, chopped
6	medium tomatoes (or one 28-ounce can unsweetened and unsalted Italian tomatoes with juice)
	Soup stock, if needed

Remove the pasta and soup mix seasonings and set aside. Rinse and soak the beans overnight in distilled water; drain. Cook and drain beans. Mince garlic. Prepare vegetables and steam sauté (or use a small amount of coconut oil) for about 5 minutes. Stir in cooked and drained beans, tomatoes, and Soup Mix. Bring to a simmer and cook about 15 minutes or until the vegetables are tender. If too thick, add more tomatoes or soup stock.

HOLIDAY MUFFIN MIX

Yield: 1 quart gift jar	
2½ cups	unbleached all-purpose flour
½ cup	whole-grain flour
¾ cup	date sugar
½ cup	non-dairy milk powder
2 tbsp.	Rumford® Baking Powder*
1 tsp.	Celtic Sea Salt®
1 tbsp.	cinnamon
½ tsp.	ground cloves

Layer ingredients in the order given into a 1-quart wide-mouth canning jar. Tap slightly after adding each layer.

Attach gift card with mixing and baking instructions.

Attach the following directions:	
1 jar	Holiday Muffin Mix
1⅓ cups	distilled water
	Egg Replacer for two eggs
½ cup	coconut oil

Preheat oven to 400 degrees. In a large bowl combine the Holiday Muffin Mix with the distilled water, Egg Replacer, and oil. Do not over mix; stir until mixture is just blended. Spoon into lecithin lined muffin tins, filling ⅔–¾ full. Bake 15–18 minutes, or until golden brown.

Rhonda's Kitchen Tips: Rumford® Baking Powder contains no aluminum, which can be potentially harmful to the body. It is available at health food stores and some grocery stores.

****Rhonda's Kitchen Tips:*** Liquid lecithin is a fairly thick pure vegetable product that forms a colloidal solution in water, and has emulsifying, wetting, and antioxidant properties. Place it on a paper towel and "grease" the baking dish, bread pan, or muffin tin, etc. Liquid lecithin is available in health food stores.

HOLIDAY FRUIT BASKET

Yield: 1 holiday gift basket

Find a beautiful gift basket then fill it with organic fruit and perhaps some unshelled nuts. Along with the fruit and nuts, add one or two of your favorite recipes using those ingredients. Perhaps a raw fruit pie recipe or smoothie recipes.

HOLIDAY VEGETABLE BASKET

Yield: 1 holiday gift basket

Find a beautiful gift basket then fill it with organic vegetables. Along with the vegetables add one or two of your favorite recipes using those ingredients. You could also add a vegetable peeler or a set of stainless steel kitchen knives. Salad Dressings for Life … from God's Garden could be added to this basket.

HOLIDAY PASTA COLANDER

Yield: 1 holiday gift colander

Purchase a stainless steel colander and fill it with a couple of your favorite organic vegetable pastas, organic spaghetti sauce, Italian Seasoning, perhaps some tongs or another utensil to serve spaghetti, and your favorite recipes.

HOLIDAY HERB TEA BASKET

Yield: 1 holiday gift basket

Is your loved one hooked on caffeine? Perhaps make a basket of organic Herb Teas along with a pretty teapot and a mug or two. You could also add some of your favorite holiday snacks. See the Holiday Delights Chapter starting on page 195 for lots of good ideas.

MAX TRIO BASKET

Yield: 1 holiday gift basket

To introduce someone you love to the Hallelujah Diet and Lifestyle℠, make up a beautiful basket that contains BarleyMax®, CarrotJuiceMax™, and BeetMax. Add a small electric mixer or small whisk along with directions on how you like to mix your Trio.

Think about adding any of the Back to the Garden Newsletters, books, audio or video CD's or tapes from Hallelujah Acres® that might be appropriate for the person you're making your gift for. Maybe even a gift certificate from Hallelujah Acres® would make a nice gift.

Be sure to put in some holiday ribbons, an ornament of the season, or perhaps a small picture of yourself or your family in a small but elegant frame for your loved one to treasure. Add something to remind him/her of you whenever he/she sees it.

HALLELUJAH ACRES® GIFT CERTIFICATES

Yield: 1 terrific gift for someone you love!

Hallelujah Acres® has gift certificates! They are available in our Health Food Store for both our café and our store. We also have gift certificates available for our life changing events, from our Culinary Academy classes to our Health Ministers training. For these certificates and a list of our events, please contact Barbie Malkmus at 704-481-1700. If you would like a gift certificate for our Lifestyle Centers, please contact each lifestyle center individually. See our website at www.hacres.com for contact information.

HOW TO PLAN A DINNER PARTY
Deborah Martin

This is just a calendar to give you ideas on how to prepare for your dinner party. Nothing is set in concrete, be creative and adjust to suit your situation.

25 days before event	Prepare formal invitations.
23 days before event	Mail invitations.
22 days before event	Plan menu.
21 days before event	Determine when items can be prepared ahead and mark planner.
18 days before event	Make list of all ingredients (including amounts).
17 days before event	Grocery shop for items that can be prepared early.
16 days before event	Make items that can be frozen.
15 days before event	Plan your table settings and centerpiece.
14 days before event	Make place cards, menu cards, party favors (a nice party favor is the recipes printed on nice paper, rolled up and tied with a ribbon).
10 days before event	Make and dehydrate items that can be stored (store in an airtight container).
9 days before event	Make piecrust and store in freezer.
8 days before event	Make a list of all the juices and grated rinds needed for recipes.
7 days before event	Make final check list of all of your ingredients needed for your recipes. Make sure you have all serving pieces needed for food.
6 days before event	Chop all nuts needed for the recipes. Store in refrigerator or freezer.
5 days before event	Bake bread for Holiday bread stuffing and store in freezer.
4 days before event	Prepare beverages that can be prepared ahead of time.
3 days before event	Prepare recipes and items that can be stored.
2 days before event	Shop for all fresh produce. Bake items that can be baked ahead of time. Prepare raw foods that can be kept well. Tidy up house.

1 day before event	Prepare foods that can be stored in the refrigerator and combined or baked the next day. Set table.
Day of the event	Prepare raw foods, so that flavors have time to mingle. Bake foods that have not been prepared ahead of time. Freshen up and prepare for guests while baking. Greet guests with a smile and enjoy the fruits of your labors!

Fresh Herbs

"For the earth which drinketh in the rain that cometh oft upon it, and bringeth forth herbs meet for them by whom it is dressed, receiveth blessing from God."

—Hebrews 6:7

Basil: (Annual) Pick leaves when young. Gather tops as flowers begin to open. Harvest early in the day. An herb that is always preferable fresh, but if fresh is not available, dried can be used. Basil is available in a wide variety of flavors from lemon to purple opal. It has a pungent flavor that has been described as a cross between cloves and licorice. Always store dried herbs in a dark place as sunlight deteriorates their freshness.

Chervil: (Annual) Gather leaves before flowering once plant reaches a height of about 4 inches. One of the classic **fines herbs** much used in the French cuisine. It has a delicate flavor and is suitable wherever parsley is used. Chop the fresh leaves into salads, dressings, soups, and sauces. If cooking, add at the end so the flavor is not lost.

Chives: (Perennial) Harvest chives leaving 1–2 inches for re-growth. Remove flowers as they open unless you want them to go to seed. An herb that enhances the flavor of even the mundane! Sprinkle them on soups, salads, sandwiches, dressings (allow to sit one hour for flavors to blend), potatoes, and cooked vegetables. Use in place of onion for a milder onion flavor.

Cilantro: (Annual) Cilantro is also called Chinese parsley (the root of the plant is ground and the spice is called Coriander). Cilantro resembles parsley in appearance except that it is pale in color. Most often used in Mexican and Asian dishes.

Coriander: (Perennial but not real hardy) Pick young leaves anytime. The roots can be dug in autumn. Collect seeds when brown but before they drop. An Old World herb is made from the carrot-like root of the Cilantro plant. It has a nutty flavor and delightful aroma. Tastes like lemon peel and sage combined. The seeds of this plant are also dried and used as a flavoring called Coriander seed. Use seed in vegetables, tomato chutney, curries, pies, cakes, biscuits, and marmalades. Use leaves in soups, sauces, salads, and even some cookies. Use stem with beans and soups. Add root to curries or use as a vegetable.

Dill: (Annual) Gather leaves when young. Pick flowering tops just as fruit begins to form. To collect seeds after flowering heads turn brown, pick stems, and hang upside down by stems in a bag to catch seeds. The leaves have a green, spicy flavor and are often used in salad dressings, sauces, or dips. Dill seeds are often dried and added to potato salads and bean soups. Ground seeds can be used for dips, sauces, and spreads.

Fennel: (Annual) Pick young leaves and stems as needed. Collect ripe seed. Fennel is a fragrant, crisp vegetable with a mild licorice-like flavor. The bulb and leaves of the Florence fennel can be eaten raw or cooked. The leaves (stalks) can be used like celery or green onions and the seeds can be ground into a seasoning to be used in sauces, breads, or crackers. Known as an excellent digestive and reputed to be used as a dieting aid.

Garlic: (Annual) Harvest like chives. Garlic is a hardy plant and member of the amaryllis family. The bulb of this plant consists of several small bulbs or cloves. Garlic has a pungent flavor that is distinctive. Fresh garlic is best, far better than powdered or pre-peeled in jars. Rub a clove around a salad bowl to subtly flavor salads. One or two cloves can be added to salad dressings or marinades for some extra flavor. The leaves of the garlic plant are also edible but have a lighter flavor than the bulbs.

Mace: (Perennial) The lacy covering of the seed from Indonesia. Mace and nutmeg are the only spices that come from the same fruit. It is orange in color, and has a sweet, warm, spicy flavor. May be interchanged with nutmeg. Cardamom also tastes similar.

Nutmeg: (Perennial) Hard, aromatic seed of East India. Used in a grated form as a spice with a warm, hardy and sweet aroma.

Oregano: (Perennial) Pick young leaves any time. If leaves are to be used for preserving, gather just before flowers open. Oregano is an aromatic herb that is a member of the mint family. The leaves of the plant are used to lend an Italian flavor to dishes such as pizza, lasagna, and spaghetti but also can be used in vegetable soups, pasta, or other dishes. Dried is more pungent that fresh.

Parsley: (Perennial) Pick leaves during the year as needed. Seeds can be collected when ripe, if desired. Parsley is an herb that is native to the Mediterranean. Parsley will have either curled leaf clusters (French) or flat compound leaves (Italian). The leaves of this culinary herb are often used as a garnish or used to add flavor. Use in juices, salads, vegetable dishes, soups (add after removing from heat), and in potatoes.

Rosemary: (Perennial) Pick small amounts all during the growing season. Gather main leaf crop before flowering. The aromatic leaf aids in digestion of fats and can be used in pates, soups, or bread or rice stuffing. Crumble dried leaves and chop fresh, or remove them before serving, as they can be tough. Try putting whole Rosemary in the oven while baking bread. Or add a sprig to an oil and vinegar mixture for a wonderful dressing.

Saffron: (Perennial) Saffron is the most precious and most expensive spice in the world! It is collected from the "Crocus Sativus Linneaus" flower.

Each flower contains only three stigmas (the part of the flower that bees pollinate). The stigmas are picked by hand and it takes more than 75,000 crocus flowers to produce just one pound of Saffron. It is bright yellow-orange and has a strong, intense flavor so it can be used sparingly.

Sage: (Perennial) Pick leaves before flowers appear. Sage is a strongly flavored, pungent herb that aids in the digestion of fats. Use in onion soup or with stewed tomatoes, herb scones, or bread.

Tarragon: (Perennial) Pick leaves any time being sure not to harvest more that ⅔ at a time to allow for new growth. The main crop should be harvested in late summer. Tarragon is one of the *fines herbs* along with chervil and parsley. Tarragon is an unusual herb with a savory flavor and a hidden tang. Use in soups, sauces, and any delicate vegetables.

Thyme: (Perennial) Pick leaves in summer; they are best when picked in early morning while plant is in bloom. Mix with parsley and bay to make bouquet garni. Add to soup stocks, marinades, bread or rice stuffing, sauces, and soups using cautiously as thyme is extra pungent when fresh. Aids digestion of fatty foods. Suits foods cooked slowly in broth.

Fines Herbs: Derived from the French, Fines Herbs is a blend of culinary herbs; either crushed or finely chopped that is added to foods during the last few minutes of cooking or just before serving. Please see Recipes For Life, chapter 25, "Herb" section, for Rhonda's version of Fines Herbs.

Bouquet Garni: From the kitchens of French Chefs, Bouquet Garni has been adopted around the world. It is a small bundle of culinary herbs tied together in cheesecloth with string or a small bag and added during the cooking of soups, stews or other savory dishes. Always remove before serving. Please see Recipes For Life, chapter 25, "Herb" section, for Rhonda's version of Fines Herbs.

Substitutions

This is a list of substitutions that should work for most recipes. It is best to avoid making more than one substitution in a single recipe.

Allspice, 1 tsp. ground: Combine ½ tsp. cinnamon and ¼ tsp. each, nutmeg and ground cloves

Amaretto, 2 tbsp.: ¼ to ½ tsp. almond extract

Apple Pie Spice: Combine 4 parts cinnamon, 1 part nutmeg, and 1 part ginger

Arrowroot, 1½ tsp: 1 tbsp. whole-grain flour or aluminum-free cornstarch

Balsamic Vinegar, 1 tbsp.: 1 tbsp. raw unfiltered apple cider vinegar

Bamboo Shoots: In cooked recipes may use asparagus

Bay Leaf, 1 whole: ¼ tsp., crushed

Bergamot Mint Bouquet Garni, 1 tsp.: Combine ½ tsp. each dried parsley flakes, dried thyme leaves, and 1 bay leaf (crushed)

Bourbon: Orange juice, pineapple juice, or peach syrup

Brandy: Organic apple juice, white grape juice, apple cider, diluted peach or apricot syrups

Bread Crumbs or whole grain cracker crumbs:
   1 slice of whole-grain bread, ground into crumbs, or quick cooking oats
   1 slice dry bread = ⅓ cup dry bread crumbs
   1 slice soft bread = ¾ cup soft bread crumbs

Brown Sugar (firmly packed), 1 cup: 1 cup date sugar plus 2 tbsp. molasses (Remember to decrease other liquid in recipe by 2 tbsp. when using this substitution.)

Buttermilk, 1 cup: 1–2 tbsp. lemon juice or raw unfiltered apple cider vinegar stirred into 1 cup non-dairy milk and allowed to stand for 5 minutes

Cake yeast, ⅝-ounce cake: 1 packet active dry yeast

Chervil, 1 tsp.: ⅛ tsp. rubbed, dried sage plus 1 tsp. dried parsley flakes

Chili sauce, 1 cup: 1 cup tomato sauce, ¼ cup date sugar, 1 tsp. raw unfiltered apple cider vinegar, ¼ tsp. cinnamon, dash of clove and allspice

Chinese black vinegar: balsamic vinegar

Chives, chopped, 2 tsp.: 2 tsp. green onion tops

Chocolate, semi-sweet, 1 ounce: 3 tbsp. carob chips, or ½ ounce unsweetened carob powder plus 1 tbsp. date sugar

Chocolate, sweet baking (German's), 4 ounces: ½ cup unsweetened carob powder plus ¼ cup date sugar

Chocolate, unsweetened, 1 ounce: 3 tbsp. unsweetened carob powder

Cinnamon, 1 tsp. ground: 1 tsp. ground cardamom or ½ tsp. ground allspice

Cocoa, unsweetened: Carob, unsweetened

Coconut milk, 2 cups: Combine 2½ cups distilled water and 2 cups shredded, unsweetened coconut and bring to a boil. Remove from heat; cool. Pour into a blender and process for 2 minutes; strain through fine cheesecloth.

Cognac: Peach, apricot, or pear juice

Cornstarch for thickening, 1 tbsp.: 2 tbsp. arrowroot starch, all-purpose flour, or 1 tbsp. potato or rice powder

Corn syrup, 1 cup: 1 cup date sugar plus ¼ cup liquid (use a liquid called for in recipe)

Cheese:

   Almond cheese or other non-dairy cheese

   Cottage cheese/Ricotta cheese

   Crumbled tofu

   Cream cheese

   Several brands of non-dairy cream cheese are available in Health Food Stores or Kosher stores

Crème de Menthe: Spearmint extract or oil of spearmint diluted with a little distilled water or grapefruit juice

Dates, 1 pound: 2½ cups pitted

Delicata squash: Butternut squash or sweet potatoes

Dill plant, fresh or dried 3 heads: 1 tbsp. dill weed

Dry red wine: Red grape juice, cranberry juice, vegetable broth

Eggs, 1 egg:

1½ tsp. powder Ener-G Egg Replacer plus 2 tbsp. water for baking and binding

½ banana, mashed plus ¼ tsp. baking powder for desserts or other sweet recipes

¼ cup soft tofu, blended with the liquid ingredients of the recipe

3 tbsp. applesauce for sweet recipes

2 tbsp. flax meal plus ⅛ tsp. baking powder and 3 tbsp. water for baking

1 tbsp. arrowroot powder or cornstarch that does not contain aluminum plus 3 tbsp. water for baking

Fines herbs: Equal parts of dried herbs with parsley and chives almost always included.

Five-spice powder: Equal parts cinnamon, cloves, fennel seeds, star anise, and Szechuan peppercorns

Flour, all-purpose, 1 cup: 1 cup plus 2 tbsp. cake flour

Flour, cake, 1 cup: 1 cup minus 2 tbsp. unbleached flour

Flour, self-rising, 1 cup: 1 cup unbleached flour plus 1½ tsp. baking powder and ½ tsp. Celtic Sea Salt®

Fresh herbs, 1 tbsp.: 1 tsp. dried herbs

Garlic, 1 clove: ⅛ tsp. garlic powder

Gelatin: Agar agar, Arrowroot

Ginger, ½ tsp. grated: ¼ tsp. ground ginger

Ginger, 1 tsp. ground: ½ tsp. ground mace plus ½ tsp. grated lemon peel

Grand marnier or orange flavored liqueur, 2 tbsp.: ½ tsp. orange extract and 2 tbsp. unsweetened orange juice

Green mangos: Sour, green cooking apples

Green or red bell pepper, 2 tbsp. chopped: Frozen bell peppers or 1 tbsp. sweet pepper flakes (let stand in liquid as directed)

Herbs, chopped, fresh 1 tbsp.: ¾–1 tsp. dried

Honey, raw unfiltered, 1 cup: 1¼ cups date sugar plus ¼ cup liquid (use a liquid called for in recipe) or maple syrup or molasses

Italian herb seasoning: Equal mixture of oregano, marjoram, thyme, basil, rosemary, and sage

Kahlua or coffee or chocolate flavored liqueur, 2 tbsp.: ½ to 1 tsp. carob powder or ½ tsp. to 1 tsp. Roma or other coffee substitute in 2 tbsp. water

Ketchup or tomato-based chili sauce, 1 cup: 1¼ cup tomato sauce plus ½ - ¾ cup date sugar and 2 tbsp. raw unfiltered apple cider vinegar, ¼ tsp. cinnamon, pinch of cloves and allspice

Kirsch: Raspberry, cherry, or currant syrup

Leeks, ½ cup sliced: ½ Green onions or shallots

Lemon grass, 1 tbsp. minced: 1 tsp. grated lemon rind

Lemon juice, 1 tsp.: ½ tsp. organic raw unfiltered apple cider vinegar

Lemon juice, 1 lemon: 3 tbsp. organic raw unfiltered apple cider vinegar

Lemon peel, 1 tsp. minced or zest of 1 lemon: 1 tsp. dry lemon peel

Light brown sugar, 1 cup: 1 cup date sugar plus 2 tbsp. unsulphered molasses

Lime, 1 medium: 1½–2 tbsp. lime juice

Mayonnaise: Rhonda's No-Oil Dressing, Vegenaise®, or Safflower Mayonnaise

Meat: Eggplant, Portobello mushroom, beans, tofu, textured vegetable protein (TVP) (NOTE: the soy products should only be used in transition or on rare occasions as they are too high in protein)

Milk: Rice milk, nut milks, or oat milk

Mint chocolate chips: In an airtight container add ⅛ tsp. of peppermint extract to a 12 oz. bag of carob chips; allow to sit for 24 hours.

Molasses: Organic maple syrup or honey

Mustard, dry, 1 tsp.: 1 tbsp. organic prepared mustard

Mustard, prepared, 1 tsp.: 1 tsp. dry mustard mixed with 2 tsp. raw unfiltered apple cider vinegar or water

Nutmeg, 1 tsp. ground: 1 tsp. ground allspice or 1 tsp. ground cloves or 1 tsp. ground mace

Oats, old fashioned rolled: Quick cooking oats

Onion, ¼ cup minced: 1 tbsp. dehydrated onion flakes (let soak in liquid as directed)

Onion, 1 medium onion: 1½ tsp. onion powder or 1 tbsp. dehydrated onion flakes

Orange peel, 1 tsp. grated: 1 tsp. dry organic orange peel

Oregano, 1 tsp.: 1 tsp. marjoram

Palm sugar: Date sugar

Parsley, 2 tbsp. minced: 1 tbsp. parsley flakes

Peppermint, dried, 1 tbsp.: ¼ cup chopped fresh mint

Pimento, 2 tbsp.: 3 tbsp. fresh red bell pepper, seeded and chopped or 1 tbsp. dried red bell pepper, rehydrated

Pine nuts: Walnuts or almonds

Port wine: Freshly extracted red grape juice

Poultry seasoning, 1 tsp.: Equal parts ground sage, thyme, oregano, and marjoram

Pumpkin pie spice, 1 tsp.: 2 tsp. cinnamon mixed with ½ tsp. ground ginger, ¼ tsp. each, nutmeg, mace, cloves

Raisins (organic): dark Organic golden currants or raisins

Rum (light or dark): Distilled water, organic pineapple juice, organic apple juice flavored with 1 tsp. almond extract

Saffron: Turmeric, for color

Seasoned rice vinegar, 1 tbsp.: 1 tbsp. raw unfiltered apple cider vinegar, ½ tsp. sugar, and pinch (⅛ tsp.) Celtic Sea Salt®

Self-rising flour, 1 cup: 1 cup all purpose flour plus 1½ tsp. baking powder and pinch (⅛ tsp. Celtic Sea Salt®)

Shallots: Red onions or Spanish onions

Sherry: Organic orange juice, pineapple juice, or peach syrup

Shortening, 1 cup: 1 cup organic unrefined coconut oil

Sour cream: Non-dairy sour cream, such as sunflower, can be made by blending the following on high until a creamy consistency is reached: 1 cup raw sunflower seeds (soaked overnight and drained), ½ cup celery juice or distilled water, juice of ½ lemon, ¼ cup chopped onion, ½ tsp. garlic powder, and ½ tsp. Celtic Sea Salt®.

Spearmint, dried, 1 tbsp.: ¼ cup fresh, chopped spearmint

Sugar, refined white: Date sugar, fruit juice, organic maple syrup, or unfiltered honey

Tomatoes, 1 can (1 lb.): 2½ cups chopped, peeled fresh tomatoes, simmered for about 10 minutes

Tomato juice, 1 cup: ½ cup tomato sauce plus ½ cup water

Tomato paste, ½ cup: ¾ cup tomato sauce cooked uncovered until reduced to ½ cup

Tomato sauce, 2 cups: ¾ cup tomato paste and ¾ cup water

Vanilla bean, 1: 1 tsp. pure vanilla extract

Vanilla extract: Grated lemon rind, orange rind, cinnamon or nutmeg combined with a small amount of the liquid called for in the recipe to make up the amount of vanilla extract called for in the recipe

Vanilla powder: 5 whole vanilla beans ground with ½ cup soft wheat berries that have been soaked 8 hours, sprouted, and dehydrated. Place ingredients in a blender and grind to a powder. Store in airtight container in the refrigerator up to three months. (Submitted by Jackie Graff, R.N., B.S.N., Raw Foods Chef)

Whipping cream (40% fat), 1 cup: Almond Whipping Cream

White wine, for cooking: Water, vegetable broth, or apple juice

Wine, red ½ cup: Apple juice for desserts and ½ cup vegetable broth for other flavorful recipes

Glossary of Ingredients

Note: If finances allow and organic is available all food should be organic.

Adzuki Beans: (Sometimes called azuki or aduki beans) Small dark red beans that are very high in protein. Native to Asia, they are now also grown in the U. S. A.

Agar agar: A natural gelatin and thickening agent made from red algae that is boiled, pressed into a gel and then dried into flakes. It contains no calories and is colorless. Agar agar is 75 percent carbohydrate and is high in a type of fiber that passes through the body undigested, adding bulk to the diet and acting as a natural laxative. Flakes dissolve in hot liquids and thicken as they cool to room temperature or below.

Agave Nectar: A sweetener extracted from the pineapple-shaped core of the Blue Agave (a cactus-like plant native to Mexico, best known for its use in making tequila). Agave is 25% sweeter than white sugar and can be used to replace honey, maple syrup, dates, stevia or other sweeteners with no aftertaste. Because it is 93% fruit sugar, it absorbs slowly into the body, decreasing the high and lows experienced with other sweeteners. In recipes calling for a cup of sweetener, use ¼ cup of Agave Nectar.

All Purpose Seasoning: A mixture of herbs used in place of salt and pepper available in local health food store. Read the ingredients to make sure there is no salt added.

Almond Butter (raw): A nut butter made from ground almonds, similar to peanut butter. Almond butter is a good alternative to peanut butter and much easier for the body to digest. Can be found in health food stores.

Amaranth: Not actually a grain but an ancient pseudo-grain originally grown in China and South and Central America; it is a member of the Pigweed family. Amaranth is now grown in the mid-west and some western states. Amaranth contains abundant protein and other nutrients like lysine, calcium, iron, potassium, phosphorus, and magnesium. The protein content is about 12-17%. Amaranth is also a good source of vitamin C and beta-carotene.

Amaranth provides a pleasant, robust, nut-like flavor when added to other foods. The most common use for "grain" amaranth is to grind it into flour for use in breads, noodles, pancakes, cereals and cookies. Amaranth is practically gluten-free. It can be use in grain-free recipes with tapioca, arrowroot, or other starchy flours to lighten baked goods. Amaranth can be popped like popcorn or flaked like oatmeal.

Apple Cider Vinegar: Vinegar made from peels and cores of apples, un-pasteurized, unheated with no chemicals added.

Arame: A thin, Black Sea vegetable with a mild flavor.

Arborio Rice: A rice from Italy with short, fat kernels. Its high starch content gives it a creamy texture when cooked.

Arrowroot Powder: A tasteless thickener powder, made from the West Indian Arrowroot plant, that is easier to digest than flour. Used as a thickener rather than cornstarch or flour to thicken soups, vegetable sautés or gravies. Blend with liquid before and add slowly while stirring to hot dishes to prevent clumps. Does not have to be heated to thicken. Most thickeners leave sauces white or cloudy, but arrowroot becomes transparent.

Arugula: A tender, mustard-flavored salad green. Leaves resemble radish leaves but have a stronger flavor.

Baking Powder: See Rumford Baking Powder

Balsamic Vinegar: An aromatic, red-brown vinegar with a sweet and sour flavor, made from the must (crushed pulp and skins) of white Trebbiano grapes and aged in wooden barrels. White balsamic vinegar is made from Italian white wine vinegar and the boiled down musts of white grapes. Balsamic Vinegar may be used if you're transitioning to the Hallelujah Diet®. However, if you're fully committed to the diet, we recommend that you use organic raw apple cider vinegar instead.

Barley: A favorite grain with ancient civilizations, it can be found mentioned in the Bible 32 times. It is a small seed produced by Hordeum, a flowering cereal plant. Even though ancient civilizations valued barley as a multi purpose food source, when the colonists brought it to the New World, it was valued for its beer brewing properties. Today Barley is the 4th largest crop of grains grown in the world. It is available today in many forms: whole, hulled, un-hulled, flakes, grits or flour. Pearled Barley is the most processed while hulled Barley is the least. Barley adds flavor to soups, casseroles, puddings, and breads, as well as many main dishes.

Barley Malt: A natural sweetener made from sprouted barley. Similar to molasses in flavor.

Basil: An herb that is always preferable fresh, but if fresh is not available, dried can be used. Basil is available in a wide variety of flavors from lemon to purple opal. It has a pungent flavor that has been described as a cross between cloves and licorice. Always store dried herbs in a dark place as sunlight deteriorates their freshness.

Basmati and Texmati Brown Rice: Basmati brown rice is an aromatic long-grain variety native to India and Pakistan. It is extremely flavorful with a tempting aroma while cooking. Texmati rice is a similar rice grown in Texas. Another similar rice, Calmati, is grown in California. Calmati looks like white rice when it is cooked. Use in Indian dishes adding spices such as cardamom, cinnamon, and cloves.

Bay Leaves: One herb that is better when dried rather than fresh. If used with parsley and thyme it can be used to make a wonderful bouquet garni. Add to marinates, soup stocks, pate, stuffing's and curries. A leaf in a storage jar of rice will lend its flavor to the rice. Add at the start of cooking and remove before serving.

Bell Peppers: Are chunky in shape and hollow inside. They are a sweet variety of pepper and come in many colors such as red, yellow, orange, brown, purple and other colors. Green bell peppers are not ripe and not recommended. When ripe, bell peppers provide a wonderful source of vitamin C.

Better Than Milk™: A non-dairy milk substitute. There are two types of Better Than Milk on the market, rice and soy, however rice is recommended. Rice milk is made from brown rice and comes in a powdered form. Can be mixed with distilled water and used in place of milk. Use in dessert recipes, pancakes, cakes, etc. that call for milk.

Bragg's Liquid Aminos™: The manufacturer claims this is a non-heated, non-fermented, non-pasteurized soy product, similar in taste and appearance to soy sauce. Recent laboratory testing has shown that there is some naturally occurring monosodium glutamate (MSG) in Bragg's Liquid Aminos that develops during processing.

Brewer's Yeast: A yeast used or suitable for brewing, a source of B complex vitamins.

Brown Rice Malt Syrup: A sweetener made from organic brown rice and naturally occurring enzymes from organic malted whole barley and water. Can be used in place of honey or maple syrup.

Buckwheat: A triangular seed produced by flowering herbs (Fagopyrum—a member of the dock family). Although buckwheat has many of the characteristics of grains, it is not truly a grain. By strict botanical definition, buckwheat classifies as a fruit, related more to rhubarb than to wheat or corn. It has a strong earthy flavor. Sometimes it is referred to as "groats" (hulled, crushed kernels) or "kasha" (roasted buckwheat groats; each is rich in taste and texture.). This makes Buckwheat a "grain" for many people who cannot eat wheat products due to allergies. Roasting adds a nutty flavor, dark color and unique aroma. Un-roasted (white) buckwheat is used with more delicately-flavored foods.

Use as a main dish, side dish, add to casseroles or soups, or grind into flour for pancakes, waffles, muffins, and breads. The flour is dark, robust, and slightly sweet, therefore Buckwheat flour is best used in combination with blander flours. Adds high quality protein, folic acid, vitamin B6, calcium, iron and other nutrients to the diet. Buckwheat has fewer calories than wheat, corn, or rice.

Bulgur: Whole-wheat kernels that have been steamed, dried and cracked.

Calimyrna Figs: Large, green-skinned figs with white flesh.

Capers: Flower buds of a Mediterranean shrub that are pickled and often used as a condiment.

Caraway Seeds: Caraway Seed is the dried fruit of the herb Carum carvi. The small, tan-brown seeds are sweet, but slightly sharp, like a blend of dill and anise. Caraway is produced in Holland and Egypt. The Dutch Caraway is a premium seed, uniform in shape, color and oil content. It is more aromatic and bitter than its Egyptian counterpart, which has a milder flavor. It's important to store your caraway seeds in the refrigerator or freezer to prolong life as they lose their flavor quickly.

Cardamom: An aromatic spice that comes in a pod containing small black seeds. The pods can be easily crushed with a mortar and pestle. Also comes ground.

Carob: A Mediterranean evergreen, member of the legume family, with clusters of red flowers. The long, leathery seedpods contain sweet edible pulp that are often dried and ground into a pulp, roasted and sold as Carob Powder. Carob and chocolate are NOT related and Carob contains none of the negatives, which Chocolate does. Ground, toasted Carob resembles chocolate powder and can be substituted in any recipe calling for chocolate.

Cayenne Pepper: An intense seasoning made from grinding small hot cayenne peppers. Caution: Very hot and can burn if too much is used; a little goes a long way.

Celtic Sea Salt®: Sea salt harvested in the northwest area of France by the 2000-year-old Celtic tradition of hand raking. Not subjected to refining and contains nearly 80 natural occurring elements as found in the sea waters.

Chervil: One of the classic fines herbs much used in French cuisine. It has a delicate flavor and is suitable wherever parsley is used. Chop the fresh leaves into salads, dressings, soups and sauces. If cooking, add at the end so the flavor is not lost.

Chives: An herb that enhances the flavor of even the mundane! Sprinkle them on soups, salads, potatoes and cooked vegetables. Use in place of onion for a milder onion flavor. Chives freeze well but do poorly when dried.

Cilantro: Also called Chinese Parsley (the root of the plant is ground and the spice is called Coriander). Cilantro resembles parsley in appearance except that it is pale in color. Most often used in Mexican and Asian dishes.

Coriander: An Old World herb made from the carrot-like root of the Cilantro plant. It has a nutty flavor and delightful aroma. Tastes like lemon peel and sage combined. The seeds of this plant are also dried and used as a flavoring called Coriander seed. Used in soups, sauces, salads and even some cookies.

Corn: Also called maize, a derivative of the early American Indian word mahiz. Corn is a very versatile plant - every part of the corn plant can be used. The husks are used for making tamales, the silk for medicinal tea, the kernels for human and animal consumption, and the stalks are often used for fodder.

Couscous: A small round pellet made from semolina flour, a traditional food of Morocco, North Africa. Made from steamed, dried and crushed durum wheat. Has a fluffy texture when prepared and can be used in place of rice in most recipes.

Cumin: A pungent, strong flavored spice (whole or ground) that aids in digestion. Used in Mexican and Indian cooking for its warm robust flavor. Use sparingly.

Currants: Seedless, dried Zante grapes that resemble small, dark raisins.

Curry Powder: A mixture of up to twenty spices, usually including cardamom, coriander, cumin and turmeric. Loses pungency quickly; buy in small amounts.

Daikon: A long, pungent white radish, with a sweet flavor. Eaten raw or cooked.

Dark Toasted Sesame Oil: Oil made from toasted sesame seeds. Dark Toasted Sesame Oil has a stronger flavor than oil made from raw sesame seeds.

Dates: The oblong fruit of the date palm. There are many varieties of dates, but three of the best varieties for food preparation are medjool, khadrawi and honey.

Date Sugar: A natural sweetener made from dried ground dates. Can be used in recipes calling for a sweetener. Date sugar has a coarse, brown texture and is not as sweet as refined sugar. Heated during processing; therefore it is not considered raw.

Dill: A European herb (Anethum graveolens) with aromatic foliage and seeds both of which are used in flavoring foods and especially pickles. Great in salad dressings, sauces or dips. The seeds are often dried and added to both potato salads and bean soups and when ground can be used for dips, sauces and spreads.

Dulse: A burgundy colored sea vegetable, with a salty taste. Wash and soak prior to adding to foods. Can also be dried and ground into flakes or a course powder. Like kelp, dulse can be found in shakers in some health food stores.

Egg Replacer: Egg substitute that is made from potato starch and tapioca flour leavening. It comes in a box and is found in the cereals or baking section of the health food store.

Elephant Garlic: A variety of garlic with very large heads however, the flavor is a little more mild. The bulbs are often streaked with purple.

Fennel: A fragrant, crisp vegetable with a mild licorice-like flavor. The bulb and leaves of the Florence fennel can be eaten raw or cooked. The leaves (stalks) can be used like celery or green onions and the seeds can be ground into a seasoning to be used in sauces, breads or crackers. Known as an excellent digestive and reputed to be used as a dieting aid.

Fennel Seeds: A good seasoning, these seeds have a licorice-like flavor, and aid in digestion.

Flax Seeds: Contain high concentrations of beneficial oils (Essential Fatty Acids). Flax seeds may be ground and used in beverages or sprinkled on salads. May also be used as a thickener or in baking as an egg substitute. ¼ cup of ground flax seeds provides 11 grams of protein.

Garbanzo Flour: A flour made from ground garbanzo beans. Available at health food stores.

Garlic: The bulb of this hardy plant consists of several small cloves. Most will recognize its distinctive aroma and pungent flavor. We recommend using fresh garlic in recipes rather than powdered or the pre-peeled varieties that come in jars. Here are some innovative suggestions for adding this versatile and heart-healthy plant to your recipe repertoire: Rub a clove around a salad bowl to subtly flavor salads. Add one or two cloves to salad dressings or marinades for extra flavor. The leaves of the garlic plant are also edible but have a lighter flavor than the bulbs.

Ginger: A reed like plant grown mostly in tropical countries. The plant's rhizome (root) is dried and ground into a powder or used fresh. Ginger has a pungent spicy flavor (a little goes a long way.) Fresh gingerroot is best stored in the refrigerator or freezer where it will keep for several months.

Herbs: Seed producing annual, bi-annual, or perennial plants used to flavor foods. Always use fresh herbs when available. Try basil, oregano, dill, tarragon, chives, mint, thyme, cilantro, fennel, garlic, Italian parsley, marjoram, rosemary, sage, gingerroot or your favorite.

Honey (raw unfiltered): A sweet liquid produced by bees from the nectar collected from flowers. Honey is a very concentrated sweetener and should not be given to babies as their digestive systems are not developed enough to digest it. If using honey, buy raw unfiltered honey from a local beekeeper. Clover and wildflower honey have the mildest flavor.

Jicama: A tan colored, beet-shaped root vegetable with crisp white flesh. Its taste is unique, similar to a cross between a pear and an apple. Can be eaten raw or cooked.

Kashi: A blend of seven grains (oats, brown rice, rye, winter wheat, triticale, buckwheat, barley plus sesame.) Can be used like rice or cooked for a cereal.

Kelp: Seaweed also known as Kombu. Can be bought in granules or sheets. Can be used as a salt replacement.

Kudzu or kuzu: A white, starchy, natural gelling and thickening agent. Made from the root of the kudzu plant that grows wild in Japan.

Lemons: Fresh lemon juice can be used to replace vinegar in most recipes. Buy fresh lemons only. Used to flavor and preserve food.

Mace: The lacy covering of the seed from Indonesia. Mace and nutmeg are the only spices that come from the same fruit. It is orange in color, and has a sweet warm, spicy flavor. May be interchanged with nutmeg. Cardamom also tastes similar.

Maple granules or sprinkles: A granulated sweetener made from pure maple syrup. Because of processing, this is not a raw food.

Matzo Meal: A whole-wheat flour available in the kosher section of supermarkets.

Medjool Dates: King of dates, they should be plump and are the largest date available. Other dates are Honey, Barhi, Kadrawi and Deglet Noor, however these are smaller and it would take at least two to equal 1 Medjool.

Millet: A protein-rich cereal grass originating in Asia and Africa and known as the "Queen of Grains." Millet is a very bland grain and is best used in combination with stronger flavors. Millet adds protein, calcium, iron, magnesium, potassium and phosphorous to the diet.

Miso: Fermented soybean paste seasoning.

Multi-Grain Flour: A mixture of various grains of flour such as unbleached white, buckwheat, rye, spelt, oat, barley or wheat gluten.

Nama Shoyu™: Traditional un-pasteurized soy sauce from Japan made from wheat. Similar in flavor to Bragg's Liquid Aminos™.

Nayonaise™: A soy-based mayonnaise substitute found in health food stores. Although it is free of egg, dairy and refined sugar, Nayonaise is not recommended on the Hallelujah Diet®.

Nutritional yeast: Golden, bright yellow, or dull brown, nutritional yeast comes in powder or flakes, and is rich in 15 minerals and B-complex Vitamins (including B-12, which is essential for vegetarians). Since it also contains 18 amino acids, it is an excellent source of complete protein. Nutritional yeast adds a cheesy taste to dishes. When using it in hot dishes make sure to add it at the end of cooking. Tastes great sprinkled on salads, main course dishes or as an ingredient in dressings.

Nutmeg: Hard, aromatic seed of East India. Used in a grated form as a spice with a warm, hardy and sweet aroma.

Oat Bran: The broken coat of the oat seed, separated from the flour.

Oat Groats: Hulled grain broken into fragments. Steel-cut oats, or Scotch oats, are made from groats that have been cut into pieces but not steamed and rolled.

Opal Basil: A variety of basil that has dark reddish-purple leaves.

Oregano: An aromatic herb that is a member of the mint family. The leaves of the plant are used to lend an Italian flavor to lasagna, spaghetti and other pasta dishes, but can also be used in vegetable soups and other recipes. Dried is more pungent than fresh.

Orzo: A rice shaped pasta, can be colored or plain.

Paprika: A red powdery condiment derived from dried, ripe sweet peppers often used to add flavor and color.

Parsley: An herb native to the Mediterranean. Parsley will have either curled leaf clusters (French) or flat compound leaves (Italian). The leaves of this culinary herb are often used as a garnish or used to add flavor.

Phyllo: Paper-thin sheets of flaky pastry dough. (Also spelled filo or fillo)

Pine Nuts (pignoli, Indian nuts or pignola): The edible soft white nut or seed from certain pinecones used primarily for sauces or dressings. Dry roasting enhances their mild pine flavor. Very short shelf life; should be stored in the freezer.

Quinoa: Pronounced "keen-wa," although not a true grain, is highly nutritious, essentially gluten-free and protein-rich. Rinse thoroughly by rubbing grains together in water in order to remove the bitter-tasting saponin. Saponin is a sticky substance on the outer part of the grain that naturally repels birds and insects. It may irritate digestion or allergies in humans.

Raisins: Deep brown with a hint of purple, sweet and chewy—raisins are made by dehydrating grapes in a process using the heat of the sun or by oven drying. It is important to always use organic raisins. Other raisins have been sprayed many times with toxic chemicals during the growing season. When they are harvested, they are left to dry which concentrates the toxins.

"Golden" raisins are those that have usually had the color removed with a bleaching agent.

Organic raisins are not sprayed with chemical poisons, therefore there is no concern about eating as many as a person may desire. Organic Thompson or Monukka varieties are usually the best.

Rice: Rice is one of the most used grains as food, around the world. There are many different varieties of rice including short grain brown rice, medium grain brown rice, long grain brown rice, sweet brown rice, just to name a few. Most people in developed countries; generally think only in terms of white rice. What they don't realize is that white rice is brown rice with the nutrient-rich bran removed. White rice is not talked about in the Hallelujah Diet® because it is not considered an option.

Rice Syrup: A thick syrup made from cracked brown rice and barley. Mildly sweet and is perfect in dishes that need a light, sweet flavor.

Rolled Oats: Hulled oats from which the bran has been removed. They have been steamed and flattened by large rollers and then baked. Rolled oats are thicker than quick cooking oats and take longer to cook. (Quick cooking oats often have added ingredients such as salt, coloring, etc. and are more processed.)

Roma: A grain beverage made from roasted malt barley and chicory that is used as a coffee substitute.

Roma Tomatoes (Italian or Plum Tomatoes): Small, pear-shaped tomatoes that are fleshy, dry and have few seeds, often used in tomato sauce or paste.

Rosemary: This aromatic leaf aids in digestion of fats and can be used in pates, soups or stuffings. Crush or crumble dried leaves, chop fresh leaves, or place dried leaves in cheesecloth to be removed before serving. If left whole, the leaves can be quite sharp in the mouth. To add flavor to bread, place whole sprigs of Rosemary in the oven while baking. Or add a sprig to an oil and vinegar mixture for a wonderful dressing.

Rumford Baking Powder: Aluminum free baking powder found in baking section of health food and regular grocery stores.

Rye: During medieval times rye was grown throughout northern Europe and the area now known as Russia. Today, most rye production is in Poland and Russia. Rye has a strong, pungent taste that some describe as bitter. It is best when used in conjunction with other cereals, such as oats. Rye can be whole, or flour, grits, or meal. Use in rye, pumpernickel, and black breads, breakfast cereals, breads, dehydrated crackers and pancakes. Rye has a 12% protein content and is low in gluten, and it provides calcium, magnesium, lysine, and potassium.

Sage: Sage is a strongly flavored, pungent herb that aids in the digestion of fats. Use in onion soup or with stewed tomatoes, herb scones or bread.

Savory (Summer or Winter): Both have a flavor similar to thyme. Winter Savory is slightly milder. Use when cooking beans or lentils or add minced leaves to soups, stews and sauces.

Scallions: A scallion is any onion that does not form a large bulb; such as green onions, shallots or leeks. Scallions are slightly milder than red, yellow or white onions. Green onions are also sometimes called spring onions.

Sea Salt: Unrefined, solar evaporated (sun-dried) sea salt; high in natural trace minerals but not sodium chloride. Contains no added chemicals. If using sea salt, choose a reputable source so that you know the salt is pure and unadulterated. Use sparingly. Note: Avoid all table salt. Most table salt is stripped of all of its nutrients and natural minerals that are then chemically added back during processing.

Semolina: Durum wheat flour, especially suitable for making pasta. Found in gourmet shops and some supermarkets.

Sesame Seed, hulled: Sesame seeds whose hulls have been removed.

Sesame Seed, un-hulled: Sesame seeds whose hulls have not been removed.

Shallots: Related to the onion and have a similar taste. Shallots consist of a small cluster of bulbs.

Shoyu: A naturally brewed salt substitute that is made of wheat. Can be used like soy sauce. Available in health food stores and Asian markets.

Sorghum: Also called "Milo" is derived from an important species of Old World tropical grasses similar to Indian corn. Sorghum is extremely resistant to drought and is grown where the climate is too hot or dry for wheat or rice to survive. With these important attributes, sorghum is a staple food grown in Africa, East Asia and India. As Milo flour or whole grains, sorghum is delicious in simple and sophisticated foods alike – pancakes, porridge, puddings, as well as main course dishes.

Soy Flour: Flour made from ground soybeans.

Spelt: An ancient cereal grain native to southern Europe. An excellent high-gluten substitute for those allergic to wheat, it can be substituted for wheat in almost every recipe. Use a bit less liquid or more flour when substituting spelt in recipes calling for wheat. Spelt contributes protein and is also full of B vitamins, such as riboflavin, niacin, and thiamin. Spelt also contains notable measures of the minerals iron and potassium.

Squash: Summer squash: crookneck, zucchini and patty-pan have edible skins. Winter squash: Acorn, Butternut and Hubbard have a non-edible hard, thick skin.

Stevia: An herb related to the daisy family that is native to Central America. Stevia extract is 300 times as sweet as table sugar without the harmful side effects of other sugar substitutes. Comes in powder or liquid form. (Please see page 16, for more information.)

Stevia Conversions:		
Sugar Amount	Equivalent Stevia Powder	Equivalent Stevia Liquid
1 cup	1 tsp.	1 tsp.
1 Tbsp.	¼ tsp.	6 to 9 drops
1 tsp.	A pinch (¹⁄₁₆ to ⅛ tsp.)	2 to 4 drops

Tahini, raw: A seed butter (thick paste) made from ground sesame seeds. It is light in color and adds flavor to soups, potato salad, spreads or even sweet treats. Can be used as a binder or egg substitute for casseroles and burgers.

Tamari: A wheat-free, un-pasteurized soy sauce. Tamari is naturally fermented in organic alcohol to preserve freshness.

Tarragon: One of the fines herbs along with chervil and parsley. Tarragon has a savory flavor and a hidden tang. Use in soups, sauces and with any delicate vegetable.

Tarragon vinegar: Raw unfiltered apple cider vinegar to which tarragon has been added and allowed to sit for several days, allowing the flavors to mingle.

Tempeh: A high protein, cultured food made from soybeans and sometimes grains.

Texturized Vegetable Protein (TVP): A dehydrated product made from extruded soy and processed into granules or chunks. Used as a meat substitute in soups and stews. Use 1 cup dry to 2 cups liquid. (Re-hydrating in tomato juice gives an appearance similar to hamburger.) Very high in protein and should be used sparingly.

Thyme: There are many types of thyme but common thyme has been used for years along with parsley and bay leaves to create a bouquet garni. Thyme stimulates the appetite and aids in the digestion of fatty foods. It has a very pungent flavor when used fresh.

Tofu (Bean Curd): Bland cheese-like substance made from soybeans or soy flour; used as a meat replacement. Tofu is very high in protein and should be used sparingly.

Tomatillos: Small, plum sized fruit that tastes like a hard, tart tomato. In their natural state they have a brownish-green husk covering light green flesh.

Triticale: A hybrid of durum wheat and rye that has a rich protein content. One source claims that triticale has more protein than either durum wheat or rye alone. It is also significantly higher in dietary fiber than wheat. Triticale may be found in whole berry form, rolled like oats, or pre-ground into flour. When using to bake yeast bread, triticale flour must be combined with a high gluten flour, such as wheat, barley, or spelt, in order to produce a loaf that isn't too heavy. Berries or rolled triticale can be used as cereal, in casseroles, or in side dishes (such as pilaf).

Udo's Choice Perfected Oil Blend™: Udo's is a cold-pressed, organic blend of oils from flax seed, sunflower seed and sesame seed—a healthy balance of omega 3 and omega 5 fatty acids. Also contains evening primrose oil, coconut oil, rice and oat germ oil and is a great source of lecithin and d-alpha tocopherol. This is not a cooking oil, so please do not heat.

Udon Noodles: A thick flat wheat noodle, similar to fettuccini.

Grapeseed Vegenaise™: A natural mayonnaise substitute found in the cold case of many health food stores. Vegenaise is free from egg and dairy and contains no refined sweeteners. Since some Vegenaise™ is made with other oils, always check the label to make sure that the product is made from grapeseed oil.

Wakame: A pale green seaweed also called alaria. Comes in sheets and gives soups, salads and other foods a delightful flavor.

Wheat Germ: The embryo of the wheat kernel separated in milling. Good source of Vitamin E and Folic Acid.

Whole Wheat: The flour from wheat berries come in two main varieties:

Hard red spring wheat—high in fiber but low in gluten—is made into pastry flour.

Hard red winter wheat—higher in protein and gluten—is ground into bread flour, which we use for baking whole wheat bread. All-purpose whole-wheat flours blend spring and winter wheat, and perform adequately in most recipes. Unlike white flour, whole-wheat flours are not treated with bleaching chemicals, and they still contain wheat germ and bran rich in Vitamins B and E. Wheat also provides protein, calcium, iron, magnesium, phosphorous, and potassium. We prefer stone-ground flours.

Whole Wheat Pastry Flour: Flour ground from soft wheat. Whole-wheat pastry flour is used for making cookies, cakes, pies, muffins, biscuits, pastries, and other foods that do not require gluten development.

Wild Rice: A rare aquatic grain of a reed-like water plant grown in the Great Lakes Region of the U.S. Harvested in earlier times from birch-bark canoes by ancient Sioux and Chippewa tribes. Wild rice was a staple in the Indian Diet, and is today one of North America's most distinguished native foods. Sometimes called the "caviar of grains" wild rice is considered a gourmet food and highly prized for its distinctive nut-like flavor.

Zest: Garnish made by using a very fine grater and grating the outer most rind of citrus fruits.

Helpful Kitchen Tips

1. To get the most juice out of fresh lemons, bring them to room temperature and roll them under your palm against the kitchen counter before squeezing, cutting, or juicing.

2. Juice lemons, limes, and oranges when in season and less expensive. Place in ice cube trays and freeze for later when you need them in recipes. One cube equals about 1 tbsp.. (Submitted by Deborah Martin)

3. Buy a good set of knives and other kitchen tools. Wash them by hand and store them so they are protected.

4. Leftover baked potatoes can be reheated by dipping them in water and baking in a 350- degree oven for about twenty minutes.

5. To easily remove burnt-on food from your skillet, simply add a drop or two of dish soap and enough water to cover bottom of pan, and bring to a boil.

6. Spray your Tupperware with nonstick cooking spray before pouring in tomato-based sauces and there won't be any stains.

7. Place onions in the freezer for four or five minutes before peeling and you'll shed no tears. The root end causes the most tears so always leave the root end on and cut it last.

8. If you accidentally over-salt a dish while it's still cooking, drop in a peeled potato and it will absorb the excess salt for an instant "fix me up."

9. When trying to open problem jars, try using latex dishwashing gloves for a non-slip grip.

10. Ripen green fruits in perforated plastic bag. The holes keeps the air in motion, yet retains the odorless gas that fruits produce to promote ripening.

11. Soak nuts and seeds (see soaking chart at end of tips section), drain, and place in dehydrator until all moisture is gone and the nuts are dry and crunchy. Vacuum seal or store in airtight container.

12. Plan ahead; find and schedule a time to plan meals, select recipes, soak nuts, make dehydrated foods so that food prep at meal time is easier.

13. After cutting an avocado and you only plan to use a portion of it, leave the pit in to help keep oxidation from happening so quickly.

14. When making an avocado salad, save the pit. Put the pit back in the salad and it will help keep the avocado from oxidation. Remove pit before serving! (Submitted by Deborah Martin)

15. How to cut an avocado: slice lengthwise around the entire avocado, and twist to separate the halves. Place the knife firmly into the center of the pit, twist and the pit will pull out with ease. You can then peel the skin off, or spoon out the pulp, or dice the avocado by cutting the flesh first horizontally and then vertically. Once you have it cut turn the avocado inside out and scrape off the flesh. (Submitted by Deborah Martin)

16. Raw potatoes will take stains off your fingers. Just slice and rub on the stain, rinse with water.

17. For ripe fruit that will not keep, wash, peel, and cut into bite size pieces. Vacuum seal or place in Zip Lock bags and place in freezer. Can be used as a snack or in smoothies, or sorbets made in the juicer, or fruit pies.

18. To eliminate the itch of a mosquito bite; try applying soap on the area, instant relief.

19. Ants will not cross a chalk line so when you see where they enter, draw the line! Or spray vinegar around door and window frames and under appliances.

20. To ripen green tomatoes or avocados, place them in a brown paper bag; close and leave at room temperature for a few days.

21. Scotch tape will remove most splinters, if applied and pulled off.

22. Take the sting out of a paper cut by washing the area, drying, and applying cinnamon.

23. A few drops of lemon juice added to simmering rice will keep the grains from sticking together.

24. If you need a ruler when out shopping, use a dollar bill; it is 6 ½ inches long.

25. Remove stickers and decals by rubbing on vinegar, allow to soak in, then wash with soap and water.

26. When making a salad, peel garlic and run it around the inside of the salad bowl to enhance the flavor of the salad.

27. When cleaning greens, especially spinach, soak in very cold water for 20 minutes; the dirt and sand will fall to the bottom of the bowl. It also makes the greens crisp. (Submitted by Deborah Martin)

28. Garlic fed to pets will act as a natural flea repellent.

29. Muffins will slip right out of the pan, if the pan is lined with liquid lecithin.

30. Before measuring honey or syrup, measure the oil first or lightly coat the measuring cup with grape seed oil and rinse in hot water.

31. A fast way to peel garlic, take clove and place it on a cutting board then place chef knife flat side down. Press with the bottom part of your hand. This will crush the garlic and the peel will fall off. (Submitted by Deborah Martin)

The Most Important Decision Of Life

Finally, let me share with you the most important decision you will ever make. Just as pure foods restore life to our physical bodies, Jesus, and only Jesus, brings life to our spiritual souls. Therefore, even though you may regain your health, live 120 years or more, there is one question for which we are all accountable. It is simply this: "What have you done with Jesus?" My friend, if you have not asked Jesus to be Lord and Master of your life and trusted Him as your personal Saviour, won't you do so today? Our Lord Jesus Christ was born, lived, shed his sinless blood as full payment for your sins, died and was buried, and rose again for your justification. By simply placing your faith and trust in Him and His shed blood alone, you can be saved and become a new creature in Christ.

"That if thou shalt confess with thy mouth the Lord Jesus, and shalt believe in thine heart that God hath raised him from the dead, thou shalt be saved. For with the heart man believeth unto righteousness; and with the mouth confession is made unto salvation."

—*Romans 10: 9, 10*

If you need more information regarding this most important decision you will ever make, please contact us at Hallelujah Acres®.

Index

Gifts To Share, 231

How To Plan A Dinner Party, 238

Fresh Herbs, 240

Substitutions, 243

Glossary, 249

Helpful Kitchen Tips, 262

The Most Important Decision Of Life, 265

Notes

Notes

Notes